SECRETS
OF THE
CUBE

Also by
the Authors

The Cube:
Keep the
Secret

HYPERION NEW YORK

SECRETS
OF THE
CUBE

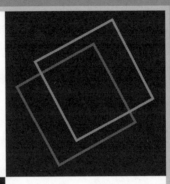

Annie Gottlieb
and
Slobodan D. Pešić

Illustrations by Andras Halasz

THE ANCIENT

VISUALIZATION

G A M E

THAT REVEALS

YOUR TRUE SELF

Library of Congress Cataloging-in-Publication Data

Gottlieb, Annie.
Secrets of the cube : the ancient visualization game that reveals your true self / Annie Gottlieb and Slobodan D. Pešić

p. cm.
ISBN 0-7868-8257-3
1. Self-perception. 2. Individuality. 3. Self-actualization (Psychology) I. Pešić, Slobodan D. II. Title.
BF697.5.S43S423 1998
158—dc21 97–41751
CIP

DESIGNED BY DEBORAH KERNER

FIRST EDITION

2 4 6 8 10 9 7 5 3 1

For both

Edward L. Bakewells, Jr. and III

and for

the Blackbird

CONTENTS

◎

◎

◎

SECRETS
OF THE
CUBE

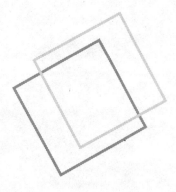

HAVE YOU BEEN CUBED YET?

BY ANNIE GOTTLIEB

That was the odd question my new neighbor asked me, right around the time new neighbors normally break the ice with "May I borrow a cup of sugar?" or (in our ancient Greenwich Village building) "Would you happen to have a plunger?"

But then, I already knew this was no ordinary neighbor.

Arrow-straight, enigmatic, svelte, sporting a single earring, dark clothing, and a Hollywood stubble, he was a filmmaker down on his luck because his country had ceased to exist. "I come from Atlantis," he explained. "I was Yugoslav; so were my friends. . . . For us the war didn't make any sense. So we left and now we feel like citizens of Atlantis." His first "artsy" film had debuted at Cannes; he had it on videocassette and would be happy to show us; and by the way, if we had a plunger . . . But first things first. If my mate and I had not been cubed yet, well, then we had to be cubed at once.

He invited us in to sit down at the kitchen table. While he made strong Balkan coffee, I had time to wonder: Was I about to be diced? Multiplied by myself twice? Given a Rubik's Cube to play with? Computer-morphed into a cubehead like the guy in the ad for disposable razors?

Slobodan (his full name means "freedom walker") set down the coffee cups, fixed us with a piercing gaze, and began, "Imagine a . . . "

Five minutes later he said, "Now I'm going to tell you what it means."

And he did.

"Son of a . . . " said Jacques, whose vocabulary for wonder is blunt and colorful.

"Unbelievable," I chimed in.

"You've just been cubed." Slobodan glowed, as if he'd pulled off a magic trick.

And in a sense he had—except that the magic is real, it lives in the depths of the human psyche, and the only trick is drawing it out. Somehow, this little exercise—innocuously labeled an "imagination game"— had led each of us to create a vivid vision, like a waking dream, that told us . . . well, but that's getting ahead of ourselves. Let's just say it told us what our Cube was. You probably know your astrological sign, and perhaps even the details of your horoscope. Now you'll definitely want to know your Cube.

We, too, started cubing everyone we knew. And our minds were blown. We began wanting to know *everybody's* cube: our grandmothers', all our ex-lovers', Bill Clinton's, Madonna's. "What *is* this thing?" we asked Sloba, by now a friend. "Where did it come from? Who dreamed it up?"

He admitted he didn't know. The Cube had simply appeared in Belgrade's coffeehouses sometime in the late eighties. Suddenly one summer all his hip artist and intellectual friends were cubing each other, but no one knew where the "game" had come from. For all they knew it might be very old, one of those fragments of folk wisdom that are never really lost but occasionally rise to the surface of the collective unconscious like a message—or a genie—in a bottle . . . from Atlantis? So for the time being we chalked it up to "origin: mysterious," though later (as you'll see in chapter 1) we would follow trails of rumor and research into the hidden history of the Cube and discover clues to its ancient and mystical lineage.

Meanwhile, even before we knew very much about it, Sloba and I wrote a little book called *The Cube: Keep the Secret*, introducing the "game" to a wider audience. And in the course of promoting that book we cubed talk-radio audiences all over the country. Commuters bored in their cars, night owls lying awake after midnight called in to describe their Cubes and ask us, "What does it mean?" For us it was an amazing experience, because of all the thousands of Cubes we encountered, we never heard the same one twice. We learned that the most demure and unobtrusive people conceal a startling creativity, that no one is "ordinary" and everybody is one of a kind. For our listeners, though, the experience must sometimes have been frustrating, because they wanted more help understanding their Cubes than we could yet give them. We were still learning.

So it's possible that you've already been cubed, and you still have unanswered questions about aspects of your Cube, or your mom's, or your boss's. If so, this book is for you. It contains the fruits of more than three years (almost ten years, in Slobodan's case) of cubing people all over the world, seeing universal patterns start to shine through the welter of individuality, and discovering how the techniques of the Cube can shed a wise and helpful light on our lives. (There are also many mysteries that remain. The Cube will not, and should not, ever be fully understood.)

Many of the problems we experience in both personal and working relationships arise because each of us sees the world and other people through a subjective filter we're hardly aware of. Instinctively seeking to structure the world according to our own needs and nature, we often fail to realize that a coworker, friend, or lover *actually lives in a different world*. When you know your Cube, you are much more aware of your own inner drama and architecture. When you know another person's Cube, you can literally see where he or she is coming from, and you have a map of that person's psyche to guide you in living or working with him or her. In the pages ahead, you'll become adept at using the Cube to understand—and reconcile—your own and others' very different but equally fascinating inner worlds.

Have you been cubed yet? If you have, you can proceed directly to chapter 1. If you don't yet know your Cube, you have a fascinating journey ahead. First prepare to get cubed! (You can also use the next section as a guide for cubing others. The questions are precisely designed to evoke maximum information without suggesting or "leading.") Then we'll reveal What It All Means, throwing open the door to a treasury of revelations.

IMAGINE A DESERT.

*** This can be a real desert you know,
one you've seen in pictures,
or a pure fantasy.**

***NOTE:**

*These questions and hints are optional, no more than prompts
for a hesitant imagination. When you're cubing someone else,
hold these in reserve and use them gently to elicit a full
picture or to answer questions like "I'm seeing the
desert around my grandmother's farm in
New Mexico. Is that OK?"*

IN THIS DESERT,
THERE IS A CUBE.

How big is the cube?

What color? What texture?

What is it made of (if you can tell)?

Is it solid or hollow (if you know)?

How far is it from you?

**Is it sitting flat on the sand, or
in some other position?**

Before you go on, write down
at least five adjectives describing your cube —
the mood it conveys as well as its physical qualities.

NOW, IN THE DESERT, THERE IS ALSO A LADDER.

What's the ladder made of?

Where is it (in relation to the cube)?

Approximately how many rungs does it have— many, several, a few?

IN THE DESERT
THERE IS ALSO A HORSE.

What kind of horse is it?

What color?

Where is it?

What is it doing?

Does it have on a saddle or bridle, or not?

If so, what kind?

SOMEWHERE IN THE DESERT IS A STORM.

What kind of storm is this?

Where do you see it?

And does it affect the cube, the ladder, and the horse, or not?

If so, how?

AND FINALLY, IN THIS DESERT THERE ARE FLOWERS.

Where are the flowers?

Are there many, or a few?

What color, what kind?

NOTES:

If you (or the person you're cubing) spontaneously add things—such as cactuses, palm trees, dunes, oases, water—then they belong in your picture. However, when you are cubing someone else, do not suggest any such additions. Simply accept those that arise.

Similarly, if the spontaneous response to "There's a horse in the desert" is "I see several horses," or "It's not a horse, it's a camel," that's fine; but as the "cuber," you must not offer such options.

If you (or someone you're cubing) simply *cannot* visualize one or more of the items, don't force it. After a couple of gentle tries, the absence of that item should be accepted as significant.

NOW TURN TO

THE NEXT PAGE

FOR THE **MASTER KEY**.

WARNING:

**Do not turn this page until
you have played the Cube!!**

THE MASTER KEY

**The Cube is you—
your symbolic self-portrait.**

**(Those adjectives you wrote down
describe yourself!)**

**The Ladder
represents your friends
and your co-workers.**

**The Horse
is your lover/life partner.**

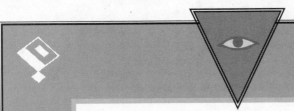

THE MASTER KEY

The Storm
is trouble/upset/challenge—
life's power to stir things up.

The Flowers
are children, of your body
and/or mind — "your baby,"
whatever you create and nurture.

The Desert
is your life, and your view of the world.

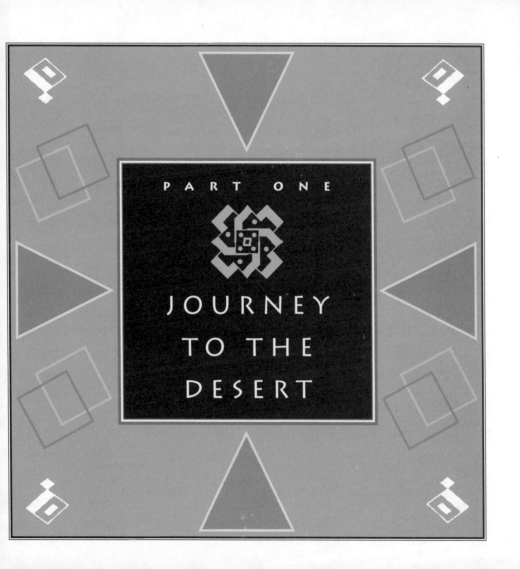

PART ONE

JOURNEY
TO THE
DESERT

CHAPTER 1

THE SECRET LANGUAGE OF THE CUBE

YOUR AUTHORS REVEALED

Now it can be told: what our own Cubes are, and why we were so blown away by the accuracy of their self-portrayal.

Ours may be the first Cubes you've seen aside from your own, so notice how completely different they are—from yours and from one another. And watch how we trace the links between our imagery and our lives, for the best way to introduce the art of Cube interpretation is to demonstrate it. We had to do it on our own—we didn't have this book!—and that's what we're going to invite *you* to do first, in this chapter, *before* we go ahead and give you a whole lot of help. Your Cube vision is so unique, specific, and detailed—more one of a kind than your horoscope—that no composite drawn from many examples can ever encompass exactly who you are. Only you hold the master key to the secrets of your own Cube.

■

Annie's desert is one she knows from the American Southwest: red sand, a bright blue sky, puffy white clouds. Her Cube, though "solid stainless steel and as big as half a house," is *floating*, bisecting the horizon so its bottom third is seen against a background of earth and the upper two thirds against sky. Its surface is brushed or chased, so it softly reflects earth, clouds, and sky.

The Ladder is smooth-sanded but unfinished white pine, simple and elegantly proportioned like the ladders in Southwest Indian pueblos. It has only three or four rungs and is floating in front of the Cube. An optical illusion makes it appear closer to the Cube, both in distance and in size, than it really is. It's actually smaller and floating closer to the viewer.

The Horse, so dark brown it's almost black, is trotting across the picture from right to left, in front of the Cube. With arched neck and tail, it's lifting its feet with such precision that it looks not quite real, like the silhouette horse on an antique iron weathervane.

The Storm is a single black cloud in the blue sky that sends down a vicious whiptail of a tornado to pursue the Horse. The little Ladder spins head over heels as the Storm passes. The Horse dodges nimbly, while the Cube simply reflects what's going on.

The Flowers are tiny and yellow, growing thickly on low, silvery, blue-green sagebrush bushes distributed randomly all over the desert.

The Cube: An absentminded daydreamer, yet one who's able to fix faucets and program the VCR, Annie recognizes herself as "floating," not down-to-earth, yet feels that "one-third earth, two-thirds sky"—the Cube's background—accurately measures the mix of cloud cuckoo land and common sense in her psyche. Steel has been toughened and refined by heat and pressure, and Annie feels that's more true of her than her closest friends know. (Remember, your Cube is first and foremost a message *for you*. Even if you played it with a group of strangers, or at a job interview, no one else would learn as much about you as you would.) The softly reflecting surface of the Cube she recognizes with chagrin: She's not revealing anything of her dense inner life these days, but is deflecting attention by flatteringly reflecting others, telling them what they want to hear. She's also feeling physically withdrawn; later it will strike her that "chased" may be a pun for "chaste." (It's important to note that your Cube reflects you *right now*. If it were "taken" at a different time, it would differ in some respects, just as photographs of you vary. But it would not be a totally different Cube.)

The Ladder: Annie has only a few girlfriends she's really close to (three or four rungs). Her closest friend is short, blond, naturally elegant, and one fourth Mexican. And though she often puts them ahead of herself, dropping everything to help out a friend in a crisis (the Ladder is more in the foreground, and is knocked spinning by the Storm), their closeness to her (the Cube) is something of an illusion. They're not really "in touch."

The Horse and the Storm: The Horse's precision trotting reminds Annie of her partner, Jacques', exacting, Austro-Hungarian military heritage. (At the same time, the Horse's slight air of antique unreality nicely reflects her past penchant for fantasy lovers—typical, as we'll see later on, of a floating Cube.) Jacques really *is* being chased by his own private Storm: At sixteen, he was imprisoned in a Soviet labor camp for two years and survived an impossible midwinter escape—memories that still pursue him like an incongruous black cloud through blue-sky America. It's a good thing he's an artful dodger, because Annie feels all she can do is watch helplessly and reflect it all. (Jacques feels very differently, as we'll soon find out.)

The Flowers: "My cats," Annie says immediately. The bushes are just about the right height and furriness. (Once she even had one called Sage.) Later on, she'll see how the Flowers could represent her work as well.

We'll tell you Jacques' cube, too, since it's instructive to see how a couple's Cubes differ, what traits they share (this pair both have Cubes made of metal), and how differently they view the same relationship.

■

Jacques is a very big guy, 6 feet 3 inches and 265 pounds, a former heavyweight fighter, so most of his friends would be surprised to learn that his Cube is smaller than Annie's (since she's 5 feet 3 inches and 120 pounds). But the size of your Cube may not reflect your physical size at all. Jacques' Cube is big enough for him to hide in (he has said that his physical size is "a disguise"). But wait: It's made of *titanium*—the super-tough metal they use for fighter jets and spy planes. In fact, Jacques' Cube is attached, by a sort of umbilical cable, to an SR-71 Blackbird, Lockheed's miraculous Mach 3+ reconnaisance aircraft (also made of titanium), which can outrace a bullet or missile and soar to a mocking 100,000 feet. Jacques' Cube is on the ground, but at a moment's notice the Blackbird can whisk it away into the stratosphere.

His Ladder is a metal fire-engine rescue ladder with endless extensions. It goes up from the Cube, into the sky and out of sight.

His Horse is a white Lipizzaner, the "dancing" horse of Vienna's Spanish Riding School.

A violent Storm comes sweeping through, with thunder and lightning, wind and rain. But the Horse outruns the storm and triumphantly escapes into a beautiful green meadow. (There are some Flowers there, too.)

The Cube: Jacques is a man of extremes—*both* extremes on any continuum—so it's quite typical that his Cube is either firmly on the ground or off in the stratosphere. He is far more grounded in the practical, material world than Annie (and gets annoyed at her obliviousness); he says being forced to survive will do that to you. But when he chooses to escape into fantasy, his departure from reality is total. And that, too, was a key to his survival. He has described lying in a cold prison-camp barracks and simultaneously being a million miles away in a favorite adventure story from his childhood.

As for titanium and the invincible SR-71 Blackbird, Annie calls Jacques "the last of the Titans." He has been connected to a series of almost superhumanly powerful men, starting with his own grandfather (who owned the land of nine Carpathian villages) and father, and including Omar, the "giant" who saved his life in a Russian mine cave-in, and world-renowned karate master Masutatsu Oyama, his teacher and close friend. He also unerringly seeks out the "titans" of literature and jazz, for the power to "save" you and lift you far above life's miseries can be artistic or imaginative as well as physical. The Blackbird is Jacques' totem, both an example and a symbol of the redeeming power of the extreme, the all but impossible.

(Mind you, Jacques didn't *know* he was doing his self-portrait!)

The Ladder: Another image for Jacques' countless friends and their lifesaving potency.

The Horse and the Storm: Annie is notorious for loving to dance. Even if she didn't, the disciplined, showy dancing of the Lipizzaner might be a good metaphor for writing. And despite her doubt that she can help Jacques dodge his demons, *he* says he sees her escaping the Storm for both of them, outracing trouble into a safe harbor of security and serenity.

The Flowers: You can tell you're dealing with non-parents here. Neither Annie nor Jacques shows the telltale sign of involved parenthood: a few bright-colored flowers in the shelter of the Cube.

■

Slobodan weighs about a hundred pounds less than Jacques, but you could fit Annie's and Jacques' Cubes together into his Cube's little toenail. "I'm seeing the Cube from way above, from outer space or something, so it's dwarfed by this minimalist desert of fine Japanese grass," he says. "But the Cube is *huge*—it's thirty miles on a side." Yes, you heard right: *miles.* Sloba has cubed the marathon. "If you see it from the ground it's an endless wall, running right, left, and up as far as you can see. It's a question of perception, of perspective. All my pictures are in two film shots." (He's a director, remember.) "It's black-Labrador granite, one of the toughest kinds of stone there is, well-polished, with very small white veins in it. You have to come very close to see them. Otherwise it just looks like an endless black wall.

"The Ladder is wooden, leaning against the Cube on the right side, and it goes all the way to the top.

"The Horse is weird. I know right away that it's not a horse, it's a mare. A big, black, beautiful mare. She comes up to this endless wall, and she's not impressed or afraid or anything. She's just, like, 'Hmmm.' It's her territory, and it's a bit of an obstacle, too big to get around, but there's no point in being angry. She kicks sand on it several times, and then . . . she *pisses* on the cube! Then she proudly leaves, not going left or right but straight away from it. Like, 'Big deal.'

"The Storm is huge—thunder, wind, clouds filling the horizon. At first I don't see the Cube, only this huge storm. The Cube has vanished. It's, like, I'm *beyond* the Cube—jumped on it, or over it. But then, in the next shot, I'm seeing that this huge storm is dwarfed by the Cube. As big as it is, if you see it next to the Cube, it's so tiny and small it's nothing."

(Alas, the friends who cubed Slobodan jumped the gun and told him what it all meant before he could get to the Flowers.)

The Cube and the Storm: Meet the megalithic ego of a film director—a profession that will prove to be mysteriously conducive to humongous Cubes. Slobodan, as a film director working in a Balkan Communist country, particularly needed the confidence, toughness, and polish to face down and stonewall anyone, to dwarf any storm. Only those closest to him could see the fine cracks in his armor, the "veins" that reveal this as a living, feeling creature and not just a wall. But as vast as his ego is, he has it in perspective; he knows that in the *really* grand scheme of things, it's pretty small.

The Ladder: "I value my friends, but they have to travel a long way, physically or mentally, to come on top of the Cube and view the world from there. Only a few have made it."

The Horse: It's all true. Slobodan is only impressed by women strong enough to be unimpressed by him.

Though we "got cubed" several years ago (over ten years ago, in Slobodan's case), we vividly remember that moment of mingled recognition and surprise that you, as a "new Cube," have just experienced—when we heard, "The Cube is you," and after a beat, we went, *"Oh, my God, it IS!"* That "beat" is a pause for translation, the time it takes to recognize familiar information in a new medium: subjectivity as an object. Somehow, this little "game" has searched out self-knowledge we didn't even know we had—from the density of our consciousness to the precise size of our self-esteem—and presented it in a form we can see and touch, at least in imagination. (Remember that episode in the original *Star Trek* when the entire *Enterprise* crew got zapped with a ray and turned into cubes?)

But why *a cube?* we wondered. Would a sphere, or an oblong slab, have done just as well? Instinctive egotists that we are, would the first object to appear in the desert—whatever it was—have had to be "me"? Or is there something about a cube that the deep mind recognizes? C. G. Jung said that the circle or sphere is an archetype, a universal symbol, for the wholeness of the Self. Might the cube also be an archetype in the collective unconscious of humanity? That would certainly explain the universal response to it. Told to imagine a cube in the desert, people all over the world create a self-portrait that they recognize as such. Only one person we've cubed, an Indian activist and screenwriter, insisted that his Cube could not be him, because for Native Americans, as in nature, everything is round. But a friend of his who heard about his Cube said, "Large, dark, out of place in the desert—he's a Chippewa in Arizona—dominating the landscape? Sounds just like him!"

This question—Is the Cube an archetype? and if so, what, exactly, does it represent?—is intertwined with another that has tantalized us: Where did this "game" originate? Who invented it? Whoever it was must have been fluent in the psyche's native "sign language" to know what meanings would reliably be summoned up by the cryptic images of a cube and a ladder. It's much easier to guess what the Horse, Storm, and Flowers stand for, even to imagine some modern psychologist coming up with those common-sense symbols; but the Cube and Ladder are far from obvious, and they have an ancient, mystical feel. In search of clues, we set out to follow the trail of the cube—as geometrical form and sacred symbol—back to the ancient world. Here's a brief tour of the cube lore we found.

(If you're impatient to find out what *your* Cube means, you can skip all this detective work for now and go straight to p. 40.)

CUBE ROOTS

THE PLATONIC SOLIDS

The Greeks learned geometry from the Egyptians, who, in turn, may have figured it out in the process of surveying the Nile floodplain (unless, of course, they got it from those extraterrestrials who allegedly built the Pyramids). In any event, geometry became a Greek obsession and glory, permeating every aspect of their culture, from architecture to religious beliefs. In the *Timaeus*, Plato's tale of the creation of the cosmos by a craftsman-god, he speculated that each of the traditional "four elements"—fire, earth, water, and air—was composed of atoms of a different geometric shape. While fire must be made of sharp, pointy little pyramids (the tetrahedron, enclosed by four equilateral triangles), Plato wrote, "Let us assign the cube to earth; for it is the most immobile of the four bodies and the most retentive of shape, and these are characteristics that must belong to the figure with the most stable faces." Other, more complex "Platonic solids" were imagined to be the building blocks of air and water.

While the ancient Greeks got the details wrong, they were right in principle: Geometric forms and mathematical formulas do resound like musical harmonies throughout the structures of matter and life. For instance, as Catherine Yronwode points out on her "Sacred Landscape" Web page, "Most fruit trees . . . have both fruit and flowers whose 'design' is clearly based on the pentagon, just as crystal usually reflects some aspect of the cube, and galaxies reflect the logarithmic spiral." To contemplate these is to tune in to "the rational beauty of the universe." "The Greeks recognized [the Platonic] solids as fundamental units of matter and thus they assumed they were related to consciousness as well," writes Tom Kenyon, a psychological counselor and director of Acoustic Brain Research. "In the ancient Greek Mystery Schools, a kind of geometric contemplation was practiced in which students . . . would alter their mental awareness (presumably in a kind of self-hypnosis) and contemplate one of the solids. By such a method, hidden (or esoteric) knowledge would be gained."

Might the Cube be a distant descendant of such an exercise? Certainly it never fails to activate the imagination with an uncanny vividness—to the great surprise of people who never thought they were especially imaginative. Were you struck by the unusual clarity of your desert scene? Kenyon, who has studied a variety of techniques for enhancing brain performance, is convinced that contemplating "sacred geometry" can stimulate intelligence and creativity, and may even be a pathway to higher consciousness. "By 'imaging' certain three-dimensional geometries in specific areas of the brain we can stimulate those areas," he writes in "Sacred Geometry and the Evolution of Consciousness," an article published on the Internet. "Imaging," Kenyon explains, is more than visualization, as it "involves other senses . . . especially feeling." As you'll see, "becoming" your Cube in imagination and "feeling" its material and position from within is vital to its interpretation.

ALTARS AND ARCHITECTURE

Speaking of "sacred geometry," squares and cubes have played a crucial role in the design of oracles, altars, shrines, mosques, and churches the world over. We know that ancient Greek altars were cubic. In classical Greece, "The cube symbolized kingship and earthly foundations . . . Thus a building dedicated to a god-king might bear traces of cubic geometry," writes Yronwode in "Sacred Landscape." In the desert of the Middle East, of course, stands the Kaaba, the shrine that is the center of Islamic worship at Mecca. Not only is the form of the Kaaba a large black cube, but its name literally means . . . "The Cube." Enshrined within the Kaaba is a meteorite, a type of stone—fallen from heaven—that had been revered as an oracle since prehistory. A similar "navel stone," set into a special (very likely cubic) base, was the holiest object at Delphi, where the words "Know thyself" were written above the entrance to the oracle. Such a shrine or oracle is a wise, otherworldly spirit enclosed in a cubic body—a crucial clue to the meaning of cubes in general.

Further east, Catherine Yronwode writes, "When Hindus (ancient and modern) plan to erect any edifice for religious purposes, from a small wayside shrine to an elaborate temple, they first perform a simple geometric construction on the ground, establishing due East and West and constructing a square therefrom." Nor has Christianity been immune to Cubism. In the Bible's Revelation 11:16, the "New Jerusalem" is described as a perfect crystal cube: "Her light was like unto a stone most precious, even like a jasper stone, clear as crystal . . . And the city lieth foursquare . . . the length and the breadth and the height of it are equal." Perhaps most intriguing, Yronwode points out that the cross-shaped ground plan of medieval cathedrals (and many modern churches) corresponds "to the form of an unfolded cube." Indeed, the pattern for folding a three-dimensional cube from a sheet of paper is a cross made of six identical squares:

In all these uses of the cube, there's a tension between the idea of perfection and the idea of earthiness, for nothing on earth can be perfect. Perhaps a cube is as close to perfection as it gets down here, and the cube symbolizes ordering and stabilizing the personality—the earthly vehicle—to make it a worthy receptacle for Spirit. Still, for medieval Christians, earth was a fallen, sinful place. The point was not to "know yourself," but to know Christ, who by his crucifixion "opened the cube" and set the spirit free from its earthly prison. If people had bothered to play the Cube back then, the game's motto would have been "Don't get to know your Cube, get out of it."

THE RENAISSANCE NEOPLATONISTS

All that changed with the dawning of the Renaissance. The revival of interest in Plato and classical antiquity swept away the medieval church's "attitude of contempt towards the visible world" in favor of the ancient Greeks' "glorification of the cosmos," according to Raymond Klibansky's *The Continuity of the Platonic Tradition*. Suddenly earth, symbolized in architecture by a square beneath a round heaven, was not a mass of sin and decay, but a substance yearning for transformation, like the *prima materia* of the alchemists. And the chief tools of transformation, the "conveyors of cosmic powers into the psyche," were images, as Frances A. Yates shows in *The Art of Memory*. The Renaissance was a veritable orgy of imagery—classical, mystical, and occult—drawn from astronomy and astrology, sacred geometry, architecture, alchemy, Rosicrucianism, and Freemasonry. The sun and moon, the planets, the four elements, the mythical bestiary, the "figure of a man with extended arms and legs [fitting] exactly into a square or circle" (a symbol of "the relation of Man to God" or of "the microcosm to the macrocosm")—such "emblems" were to be contemplated for the express purpose of self-transformation.

It's within this context that we find the first (to our knowledge) explicit depiction of a cube as a symbol for a person:

The Newberry Library, Chicago

This engraving from the English poet George Wither's 1635 *A Collection of Emblemes* is titled "The figure of the perfect man." It is reprinted in *The Architecture of Paradise* by William Alexander McClung, who remarks on "the square as symbol of . . . moral perfection" and on Wither's cube as "a symbol of the perfect man who will become a building block of the spiritual temple." It's perfect because, in McClung's words, "the identical appearance presented by the cube, 'wherever borne,' figures the constant soul, however tossed."

Note, however, that this cube is in no position to be used as a building block. It is, rather, in a position we would identify, if we were interpreting this Cube, as belonging to someone who is both a Perfectionist and a Visionary! Discovering this image was a striking confirmation of two of our "Seven Key Positions" (see page 65), which we had to reconstruct from the raw evidence of actual Cubes, since any tradition of Cube interpretation has been lost.

But that there *was* such a tradition, we are convinced. Renaissance "emblems" were drawn from existing classical and occult sources. George Wither got his idea of the cube as a symbol of the "constant soul" *from* somewhere. Possibly, as the notion of a "building block" hints, he got it from the mystical secret society of Freemasons. And one line of speculation traces the Masons' secret transmission back to some likely Cube suspects who actually lived in the desert: the Sufis. (One Sufi brotherhood was called "the Builders.")

THE SUFIS AND THE ENNEAGRAM

Sufism is commonly thought to be the mystical heart of Islam, as the kabbalah is of Judaism, but according to poet Robert Graves, "the Sufis are at home in all religions." They simply coexisted in space and time with the rise of Islam, and were fairly hospitably sheltered by the Saracen, Moorish, and Ottoman empires between A.D. 800 and 1800. But Sufi influence spread far beyond Islam, from the deserts of the Middle East and North Africa into Spain and Ireland in the west and Afghanistan, India, and China to the east. "Sufism is believed by its followers to be the inner, 'secret' teaching that is concealed within every religion," wrote the late Idries Shah in *The Sufis*. The doorway to that teaching is the realization that "Man is not as free as he thinks he is . . . he is, largely, a bundle of what are nowadays called conditionings—fixed ideas and prejudices, automatic responses . . . " Sufi methods for awakening from conditioning have included meditation, physical movement exercises, ecstatic dance, letter and number contemplation, sacred geometry, parables, puns, practical jokes, and funny stories about the misadventures of a character named Mulla Nasrudin.

While we can't prove that the Sufis invented the Cube, we think it has their fingerprints all over it. The first and biggest thumbprint is "Imagine a desert." There are no deserts in Yugoslavia, where the game most recently cropped up. But there surely were Sufis there during the five-hundred-year Ottoman occupation, who came in from Turkey (still a major center of Sufi activity) bringing the memory and culture of the desert with them. Then, too, there are multiple Sufi associations with squares and cubes. Idries Shah hints that the rebuilding of the Kaaba in A.D. 608 may symbolize the "rebuilding . . . of spiritual man from his ruined state." He also shows how, when a particular Mason's mark is drawn on a "magic square" containing the numbers one through nine in a particular order, the only number left free is eight—"the number of perfect expression . . . representing, among other things, the cube . . . The meaning here is 'The eight (balance) is the way to the nine' . . . whose hidden meaning is 'secret knowledge.' "

Once again, balancing or "cubing" the personality clears the way for higher evolution.

Finally, the Sufis have always shown a willingness to use apparently playful or merely "psychological" devices, which can be enjoyed on many levels of understanding, to provoke spiritual development. The Mulla Nasrudin "jokes"—really short teaching stories disguised in slapstick absurdity—are

one example. Another is the elegant piece of sacred geometry called the Enneagram, the system of nine interlocking personality types, which is believed to be of Sufi origin. As a tool for self-understanding that can be played as a parlor game, the Cube has affinities with both.

The Enneagram was introduced to the West by students of the Greek-Armenian teacher G. I. Gurdjieff. The author of *Meetings with Remarkable Men* had spent his young adulthood traveling through the Middle East and Central Asia, and he certainly fits Idries Shah's definition of a Sufi. The first principle of Gurdjieff's spiritual training, which he starkly called "The Work," was "Know Yourself"—the same words engraved over the entrance to the Delphic Oracle. Gurdjieff didn't mean "know yourself" in a fun, magazine-horoscope way. "The Work" was (and is) challenging and difficult: Watch how you're conditioned, fragmented, false, automatic; study the trap of your personality type in order to loosen its grip. But today, the Enneagram is also widely used as a psychological tool to improve self-understanding and interpersonal understanding in relationships and at work. And even people who don't follow it to its higher altitudes of spiritual development are, just by using it, developing— becoming more self-aware.

The same is true of the Cube. It's curious and appealing to meet this mysterious, rather lovely alter ego, bearing good news of your uniqueness and creativity. If anything, your Cube is more seductive than your Enneagram number because it's less intellectual, more sensuous, and more individual. (Your Cube is the only one like it on earth.) But once you've seen it, you can't unsee it, and it starts you thinking . . . about your tendency to reflect others, or your hardness, or your lack of boundaries, or your standoffishness. Your Cube shows you these things objectively, without judgment. You see that they have been your way of surviving; you see how they work, and how they don't work. Options and choices open up. And the Cube does all this very gently. It's subtle. It's sneaky. We think it's Sufi.

CLAUDE BRAGDON

"Man is a Cube, crucified in Time." Reading those words, written by an eminent twentieth-century architect and theosophist, startled us more than anything since George Wither's engraving of "the perfect man." We suddenly felt we were close, very close, to discovering the true ancestry and meaning of the Cube.

Rochester, New York, native Claude Fayette Bragdon (1866–1946), a member of the Prairie School of American architecture, was a friend of Louis Sullivan and the designer of Rochester's Grand Central railroad station, as well as a number of handsome houses and churches in his hometown. Bragdon was also an active member of the Theosophical Society, the "worldwide association dedicated to practical realization of the oneness of all life and to independent spiritual search," founded in 1875 by H. P. Blavatsky. At Olcott, the estate that serves as the American Theosophical Society's headquarters in Illinois, the main entrance gate was designed by Bragdon; its "pillars are capped by two of the five Platonic solids, symbolizing the order inherent in the universe." In his book *Dynamic Symmetry,* we discovered that Bragdon's views on art, architecture, mathematics, and the quest for self-knowledge precisely paralleled our research into the roots of the Cube:

Mathematics has always been deeply involved with the esotericism of every religion and was ever considered to be a sacred science. The letters of the Hebrew alphabet had each its numerical equivalent and spelled meanings to the initiated more profound than any contained in the texts themselves. Euclid derived his geometry from the priests of Egypt, and the contribution of Pythagoras to the science of mathematics was a mere by-product of his religious philosophy founded upon mathematics and now lost to the world.

> . . . *The pyramids of Egypt are less the work of the artist than the geometer . . . An amazing mathematical esotericism lay behind Greek architecture, the same which lay behind that of Egypt. Some of this the Romans in turn inherited from the Greeks and in the form of masonic secrets it descended through the Commacini builders in the north of Italy to those mediaeval guilds of freemasons which built the great cathedrals wherein, with new eloquence, the fact is proclaimed that "God geometrizes"—Gothic architecture being indeed . . . mathematics made palpable. That the Moors were amazing mathematicians is written large in their architecture and their ornament, and mathematics is a great factor in the art of the Chinese, Japanese and Hindus. . . .*
>
> *The consciousness which has produced modern industrialism is centrifugal: it seeks some center outside of itself—in the Not-I. It says, "I will acquire." The consciousness which produced that serene and austere beauty which we so admire found its center in itself. It said, "I will become." On the lintel of the temples was engraved the legend ("Know thyself!"). The corresponding modern dictum might very well be, "I know all save myself alone."*

Bragdon was a modern "Renaissance man" of many artistic and philosophical interests. Not only an architect, but a writer, cartoonist, draftsman, illustrator, poster artist, and stage designer, he also experimented with "color music," collaborating in the invention of the "clavilux," or color organ, an instrument that projected "lumia," or changing, abstract plays of colored light. But the nexus of his interests lay at the very crossroads of spirituality, geometry, and self-discovery where the Cube stands as a gatepost. Bragdon wrote admiringly of Dane Rudhyar, author of *The Astrology of Per-*

sonality. He himself used the term "personality tracings" for the changing patterns made on the surface of a plane by a solid passing through it. Excited by the coming together of science and spirituality, Bragdon believed that "higher space"—the hypothetical fourth dimension and beyond—might well prove to be identical with higher consciousness. To illustrate what it means to be a four-dimensional being whose body and senses are confined to three dimensions, Bragdon brought it all down a notch, showing how beings who are really cubes, but don't know it, would perceive themselves in a two-dimensional plane world. The result is a parable, "Man the Square," included in his book *A Primer of Higher Space*.

Cube beings intersecting a plane at random angles would not, of course, appear in the plane world as perfect squares. Rather, "each individual traces in the film world a different figure, determined by the angle at which it meets the film—*by its attitude toward life*." Only those lopsided polygons who worked hard to orient themselves correctly to their two-dimensional reality would rediscover their birthright angles and get squared away. And the purpose of such inner work is that these more conscious and rectified personalities would have the best chance of dimly intuiting their true cube nature. Still, Bragdon wrote, "The cube is the true individual, of which the square is but a single illusory and inadequate image."

It follows, of course, by restoring the missing dimension, that in our world of 3-D space, it is the *cube* that represents the earthly personality, that "illusory and inadequate image" of the "true individual," which in turn is symbolized by "a solid of the higher-dimensional space beyond your perception"—a *four*-dimensional hypercube, or tesseract. Of course, just seeing yourself *as a cube* is already a step in the right direction. Remember, we surmised that "the cube symbolizes ordering and stabilizing the personality—the earthly vehicle—to make it a worthy receptacle for Spirit." Perhaps learning the lessons of your Cube, or even just "imaging" and contemplating yourself-as-a-cube (as in those Greek mystery schools), helps to balance and orient you so that you can tune in to higher dimensions. But Bragdon makes it clear beyond a doubt that the cube—with its unique position, size, and material—*is* a symbol of personality, the manifestation of soul in the three-dimensional world.

It's almost impossible to believe that Claude Bragdon never played the Cube.

LEARNING *YOUR* PSYCHE'S LANGUAGE

So the case for the cube as the archetype of the earthly, embodied personality is a strong one. But it's even more specific than that. A personality, like a cube, has an inside and an outside. There's what Jung called the "persona," the face you present to the world, and then there's your inner sense of "me," your habitual thoughts, moods, and attitudes. As an object with a surface and an interior, your Cube portrays both—how you appear and how you feel to yourself—and reveals whether they are in sync or at odds. Are you what you appear to be? Or is your surface a concealing shield, a dazzling high gloss, or a brilliant disguise? What's really remarkable about playing the Cube is discovering how much we know about ourselves, inside and out.

The symbolism of the ladder is a subject we'll address when we come to the chapter on Ladders (see page 203). For now, it's enough to say that when a woman with a steel Ladder tells us her best friend's last name is Steele, and when a Ladder with a broken, rotted rung belongs to a man whose best friend drowned, we are convinced that our putative Sufis knew what they were doing. Horse, Storm, and Flowers are symbols anyone can understand and might even consciously choose to represent Lover, Trouble, and Children (of the body or mind).

We can have confidence, then, that each basic image in the game is archetypal—and indeed, everyone seems to recognize at a deeper than conscious level what these images mean. Each one acts as an irresistible invitation to project the corresponding aspect of your life. And so the instructions of the game are deliberately designed to create a waking dream *in anyone* that is a "life study" of that person's self and world. This is true for people from every culture and continent. (We know, because we've played it with people from all over the world.) These five symbols (six, counting the desert) seem to be universal. Like scientists working on the human genome project, we've decoded a segment of the psyche's native language.

Moving into the particulars, however—your Cube's position and material, its relationship to the Ladder and Horse, and so on—we find that no two visions are alike. And so the question arises: Where is the line between the universal and the individual, between the "collective unconscious" and the personal unconscious with its own private language of symbols? That question has a practical sister: How much help can we, or anyone, give you in interpreting your Cube and those of the people you know? All right, so the Cube is the personality. But does an aluminum Cube, let's say, always represent the same *kind* of personality? Or does aluminum mean completely different things to different people?

By now we've heard the Cubes of thousands of people, and we can tell you that the answer lies somewhere in the middle. On the one hand, there's no question that certain personality traits *are* consistently associated with certain positions or materials of the Cube. When the last five people you've met who have aluminum Cubes are all tough, adventurous, and cynical, it starts to get pretty convincing. We've gathered together all the emerging patterns we've seen, and we're going to share them with you in the rest of this book, because they'll almost certainly help you to get a handle on your own Cube. *But these meanings must not be taken as gospel,* nor are they the last word or the whole story on your Cube. They're offered only as a launching pad for your own explorations. We'll also have done our job if our interpretation of your Cube provokes you to say, "No! It's *not* that—it's *this*."

Cube interpretation is like dream interpretation: Finally, no one else can tell you authoritatively what a dream of yours means, because it's composed from sources so unique and private that only you can track them down. There are common symbols, surely, but there are also countless, subtle variations on them—*and* there are exceptions to them. (As Freud said, sometimes a cigar is just a cigar!) A man we know whose Cube is a house with aluminum siding is unpretentious and domestic, not tough and cynical. A Cube balancing on one corner may strike you as wobbly and precarious, but to someone else it will be exquisitely poised. A psychic image has its "meaning" (which is never simple *or* single) only within its total context.

"My procedure is not so convenient as the popular decoding method which translates any given piece of a dream's content by a fixed key," Freud wrote in his classic *The Interpretation of Dreams.* "I, on the contrary, am prepared to find that the same piece of content may conceal a different meaning when it occurs in various people or in various contexts . . . the same dream-element [or Cube element] will have a different meaning for a rich man, a married man, or, let us say, an orator, from what it has for a poor man, a bachelor or a merchant." (Or a woman. Though we have to admit that, when we're asked if we can tell a person's sex from their Cube, the answer is no. Maybe, *maybe* we could tell from their Horse, as you'll see when you get to the Horse chapter.)

Dream interpreters among the Arabs of the Middle East knew the importance of context well, according to a French-Swiss missionary whom Freud quotes: "In order to give a precise interpretation of a dream, the most skillful dream-diviners [*oneiromanciens*] find out from those who consult them all the circumstances which they consider essential in order to arrive at a right explanation. . . . Among these enquiries are habitually included questions as to the dreamer's closest family relations—his parents, wife and children . . . " To have a chance of interpreting your personal Cube vision really accurately, in other words, we would need to know you, or would at least need to learn something about you. Without that, we can't place your Cube within its full context—*but you can*. That's why we suggest you stop now (if you haven't already) and explore your Cube vision on your own before you read on.

There is a beautiful Arabic Sufi word for the art of interpreting soul images: *ta'wil*. Some of us already do this as easily as breathing. Others feel hesitant and unsure in the surreal landscape of the psyche. Especially if you rarely remember or understand your dreams, your Cube images may seem to be in a foreign language. Are you having trouble seeing how your Desert, Cube, Ladder, Horse, Storm, and Flowers relate to your life? Try the following four techniques.

1. Free-Associate. This was Freud's brilliant discovery of a method for interpreting dreams, and it works equally well for interpreting Cubes (further evidence that they're "composed" in the same language). No one can give better instructions than the master himself: "My patients were pledged to communicate to me every idea or thought that occurred to them in connection with . . . their dreams. . . . This involves some psychological preparation . . . We must aim at bringing about two changes in [the dreamer]: an increase in the attention he pays to his own psychical perceptions and the elimination of the criticism by which he normally sifts the thoughts that occur to him. . . . It is necessary to insist explicitly on his renouncing all criticism of the thoughts that he perceives . . . reporting whatever comes into his head and not being misled, for instance, into suppressing an idea because it strikes him as unimportant or irrelevant or because it seems to him meaningless. . . . If he succeeds in doing this, innumerable ideas come into his consciousness of which he could otherwise never have got hold." Freud cautioned that it wasn't possible to free-associate to a whole dream at once; it had to be done image by image.

Look at any part or detail of your Cube vision. What comes into your head, even if it seems unrelated or nonsensical? Let your thoughts wander freely, and you'll uncover vital clues to the meaning of that element. When we cubed country-music star Joe Diffie for our first book, this is how he described his Ladder:

"Well, the first thing comes to my mind is that old movie, with Jimmy Stewart in it? And they had a ladder on an airplane that was crashed in the desert, and they were trying to fix the plane up? I forgot the name of the movie, but . . . it's just sitting on an airplane that's half-covered with wind-blown sand, and the ladder's up on the wing. It had red on the sides, and silver rungs. . . . It's closer to me than the cube is and to the right."

When we revealed the answers, Diffie said, "The ladder is my friends? Huh! *That's* wild. Now what does that signify, that I had it next to an airplane?"

"You tell us," we said, as stone-faced as Sphinxes.

"Well . . . maybe I relate to that 'cause it involves a team, a bunch of people workin' on this airplane, trying to get it to fly. It takes everybody with different skills, trying to do their part on the airplane to make it fly."

"So that's what it's like when you do a record or a tour?" we asked.

"Yeah! *Exactly.*"

2. Look for verbal and visual puns. We noted that puns and word-play are "technologies of the sacred" in the mystical traditions of the Middle East, playing an important part in both Sufism and the kabbalah. Freud discovered that they're prominent in the language of dreams as well, and he explicitly connected the two: "[T]he oriental 'dream-books' (of which ours are wretched imitations) base the greater number of their interpretations of dream elements upon similarity of sounds and resemblance between words. The fact that these connections inevitably disappear in translation accounts for the unintelligibility of the renderings in our own popular dream-books. The extraordinarily important part played by punning and verbal quibbles in the ancient civilizations of the East may be studied in the writings of Hugo Winckler [a famous archeologist]." Apparently, the soul experiences a similarity between two words' sounds as a kinship of meaning, and will use this method to send very subtle and sophisticated messages. Scanning your desert scene for puns may turn up discoveries like Annie's realization that the "chased" surface of her Cube could also mean "chaste" (but only on the surface!).

Puns can also be visual. A "blue" Cube may be saying that you're sad or depressed. A flying Horse has been known to represent a lover who is, at that very moment, on an airplane.

3. Use your kinesthetic sense. Don't trust your "mind's eye" only. The body is very smart and is hot-wired to your intuition. The way your Cube *looks* will tell you about your outward persona, but the way it *feels* is the texture of your subjectivity, and the similarity or contrast between the two reveals how much *you* reveal of your inner self.

Imagine that you *are* your Cube. (You are!) How does it feel to be that Cube? Consider its *position:* Do you feel stable? Teetery? Up in the air? Dug in? Hidden? On display? And what about *size?* Do you feel small and insignificant in the vast desert, or do you feel rather . . . monumental? Is your *material* dense inside, or open, light, and airy? Cold? Warm? Can light get inside? Can people see into you? Is the real action in your desert "in here," or "out there"? Does the Ladder give you a firm feeling of support, or is it leaning on you too heavily, or clinging uselessly? Or is it standing off by itself? At just the right distance, or would you like it to be closer? And what about the Horse?

We'll ask these questions again, and many others, when we start to talk about each image in detail. As you become aware of any physical quality of your Cube, Ladder, Horse, Storm, or Flowers, even if you can't put it into words, free-associate directly to that feeling. See what it brings to mind.

4. Ask family and friends. The people who know you well already know the context of your life, so after yourself, they're the best Cube interpreters you can have. They won't see everything you see, but they may notice something you've missed.

The Cube—the game—has an "inside" and an "outside," too. It's most fun and fascinating to play with others so you can compare and contrast. Do play it with family, friends, coworkers, workshop participants, or even strangers at a party. You'll find it shifts the ground of conversation and interaction to a new, fresh place, neither as banal as small talk nor as intimate as personal confession. And yet, your Cube preserves your privacy. Its revelations to others are strictly limited. In the final analysis, as your dreams are, it's a secret message from you to yourself.

CHAPTER 2

SECRETS OF
THE DESERT

Why does the Cube make its appearance in a desert, and not in a meadow or a forest? Aside from the game's likely origin in the Middle East, the obvious answer is that a desert gives good background. Because it's spare, it offers a minimum of distraction from the elements placed in it.

At first, we gave no more thought to the desert than that, assuming (apologies to all you desertologists out there) that it was just the closest thing in nature to a blank canvas. Then someone jolted us with the question, "But what does the *desert* represent?" And the question kept recurring. Finally we had to sit up and notice that people imagine their desert landscapes just as individually as they do all the other elements in the game. Your desert is, of course, an integral part of your Cube vision.

Some people, it's true, treat it as a mere background, like we did, and hardly mention it at all. That in itself is probably revealing of their (our) approach to life. People who are good at isolating figures from their backgrounds are said by cognitive psychologists to be "field independent," a style of being, thinking, and working that is analytical, self-motivated, and left brain. "Field dependent" people, by contrast—those who see the background as vividly as the figures and don't strongly distinguish between them—are said to have a more "global," right-brain, and people-oriented style. At work, they would be less self-sufficient, more responsive to human feedback, and while they might lack the field independent person's laserlike focus, they would have better "peripheral vision" for subtle but significant background detail. (Not to mention that they'd be better at playing "Where's Waldo?") "The Cube" could almost be a distant cousin of the GEFT, or Group Embedded Figures Test, that psychologists use to measure field (in)dependence—"desert awareness" being the crucial variable.

Since about 70 percent of people appear to be more field dependent, it's hardly surprising that most of us, as we visualize the Cube, Ladder, Horse, Storm, and Flowers, also refer to various features of the landscape in which—and *with* which—our images interact. For instance, when you heard "There's a ladder in the desert," did you immediately provide it with a palm tree or a cliff to lean on? Some people do. And clearly, they have a different outlook on life and friendship than someone who rests the ladder against the Cube—or expects it to stand on its own.

That's a detail we'll examine more closely when we come to friends and ladders. Right now we have broader questions to ask: What *does* the desert mean, anyway? And what do we give away about ourselves by the way we picture it?

THIS IS YOUR LIFE

The desert sets the scene for your psyche's drama. Like a stage set, it creates a mood and an atmosphere—with its weather, landforms, light, and colors—even before the first actor, your Cube, comes onstage. And like a stage set, you've noticed, it changes as the drama unfolds and each "character" appears on the scene: Your desert may be animated by the entrance of the Horse, darkened by the Storm, cheered by the Flowers. Like a stage set, too, the desert sometimes furnishes props, aids, and obstacles (such as cacti, dunes, oases, or mirages) that play active parts in the drama.

We've tried saying "The desert is the world," but clearly it's a very subjective world—the world as *you* see it. Is it a hospitable and helpful place, with plenty of water, shade, nourishment, and support? Or is it hostile or indifferent, a bare expanse of sand, perhaps studded with prickly cacti? Is it level and monotonous—or would you rather say serene? Or is it a dramatic landscape of ups and downs—cliffs, mountains, gullies? What time of day or night is it in your desert? What about the softness or harshness of the sand, the play of light and shadow?

This is much more than just "your environment" or "your situation"— though it is those. Your own temperament, habitual outlook, and current mood are thoroughly mixed into it. So perhaps it would be more accurate to say, **"The desert is your life."**

Can you sum up the feel of *your* desert in a single word? (Some of those we've heard are: comfort, hardship, romance, drama, fun, adventure, boredom, sadness, mystery, challenge.) There you have the leitmotif of your life as you see it now. It is a view of life, as you may be aware, that both *reflects* your circumstances and *affects* them. Someone who pictures the desert as a lush, hospitable place with lots of water is obviously more optimistic and complaisant than someone who sees it as harsh and forbidding—and even though each outlook may be based on experience, it also tends to become a self-fulfilling prophecy. Go-it-alone people often overlook sources of aid and support that are there, all the while bitterly (and accurately) observing that those who've enjoyed life's blessings seem to keep attracting more of them.

Seeing how differently other people portray the desert, and how that matches the tenor of their lives, is a wake-up call. It shows that your own view of life is deeply characteristic of you—but not the only way to look at life. Once you've seen that people can install hot and cold running water in their deserts if they feel like it (one enterprising actress even covered hers with an Astrodome), you realize that the power to make things happen really *does* begin in belief and attitude. Shaped by the interplay of event and temperament, your attitude toward life by now has hardened into habit; but once awareness enters, it becomes a choice. You may choose to accept your existing view of life, but you can never again deny that the choice is yours.

So, is this going to be one of those books that tells you how to take charge of your life, make your dreams come true, visualize goals and achieve them? Are we going to make this into an exercise: Change Your Desert, Change Your Life? The mind is so mysteriously powerful, it would probably work: Plant and irrigate your imaginary desert, put in whatever it would take to make it the most nurturing place on earth for you, and you might well find yourself emboldened and freed to make the corresponding changes in your life. Who wouldn't want to do that?

Well . . . some people think the desert is just fine the way it is, even in its bleakness. And just because their attitude is out of fashion in these go-for-it times, we want to put in a good word for *them,* too.

Stoic acceptance of one's fate, of the hand one has been dealt, has been admired as a noble attitude in many times and places. It's not just a bunch of sour grapes to be tossed out now that technology and affluence have made it easier to fulfill our wishes. As powerful as the human mind unquestionably is, it has a worthy and wily opponent in life, and some people find it more awesome to be life's creations than to be its creators. (In practice, of course, most of us strike a balance between the two.) Whether they acquired their fatalism through difficult or tragic events, or whether their fatalism laid them open to such events, it has given them a gravity that they may choose not to trade for gratification.

The Cube gives you a good look at your life. What to do about it, or not, is up to you.

DESERT DECOR

Nothing you put into your desert is there by accident. It's all there for a reason. And while that reason may well be unique and personal to you, some common patterns have declared themselves over our years of cubing. If any of the following features shows up in your desert, you can be fairly confident of what it means. (As always, though, follow your own trail of associations first.)

Cacti almost invariably represent . . . **difficult people**. They may stand for other kinds of difficulties, too, but their prickly, humanoid shape and size seems to make this an irresistible metaphor. If your Cube is surrounded by cacti, take a look around you. We'll bet dysfunctional family members, balky coworkers, or irascible friends are an inescapable part of your present life.

We know one man—loyal brother to a brilliant, hard-drinking artist and friend to many more of that breed—whose Ladder was actually *made* of cactus. In a more common and poignant variation, we find that when the Flowers (children) grow on cacti, there has almost always been a divorce. And God knows, remarriage can land you in a veritable cactus patch of exes, in-laws and outlaws, and stepchildren.

Palm trees portray **sources of support, shelter, and nourishment.** They usually appear on the scene to prop up the Ladder or give shade to the Flowers (occasionally the Flowers will even grow on the tree), indicating that others are protected and provided for without the Cube (you!) having to do it all. The palm tree thus suggests a blessed freedom from overanxious responsibility, worry, and insecurity—a trust in providence, or in life. Call it the tree of life, plenteous source of food and shelter. Or be cynical and call it the money tree (as in Palm Springs, Palm Beach . . .). One or more palm trees in your desert can signify affluence, faith in the abundance of the universe, or someone or something that is a "tree of life" for you.

Water in the desert most commonly represents **emotional nourishment**—the presence of feeling or love. People sometimes portray their family as an oasis, their Horse grazing on vegetation fed by a spring or pool, or their Flowers as water lilies, floating on love. Conversely, a hungry, thirsty Horse in a parched desert is a warning signal: Your lover needs more affection and attention! Some see the Storm as a source of water; they are people who like to fight and make up, who feel relationships are renewed by clearing the air, or who have grown closer to loved ones through trouble. A New Age book editor we know saw the desert as a beach, complete with ocean. *That* much water could only signify universal love, the collective unconscious (two themes of the books she publishes) . . . or the fervent belief that "Life's a beach."

Mirages—no surprise here—represent "life's **illusions**," like the clouds in the Judy Collins song "Both Sides Now." Their presence in your desert may simply mean you enjoy the shimmer of fantasy and mystery for its own sake. But they can also suggest something darker: that you doubt your hopes and dreams will really come true. Perhaps you've been disappointed, disillusioned, or tricked in the past, and you mistrust alluring new prospects, fearing they too will dissolve into heat waves if you come too close.

Dunes are highly suggestive of **sensuality**. And it's not just that sexy sixties Japanese art movie, *Woman in the Dunes*. It's that women "R" the dunes. It's a cliché of landscape photography that those soft, pillowy curves look just like flesh. (Must be why "dune" and "nude" are anagrams of each other.) Dunes in your desert can signify a satisfying love life, or pleasure in your senses. But they could also say you see the world as soft, welcoming—almost motherly.

Mountains, by contrast, invoke **spirituality**. Snow-capped peaks on your desert's horizon indicate that you choose to keep a spiritual perspective in sight. You've had transcendent experiences, or sought out spiritual training, and spirit has become a permanent, protective presence in your life.

Cliffs and gullies: Rugged terrain, with lots of ups and downs, suggests either **dramatic events** or **emotional highs and lows**. This kind of desert belongs to someone who has strong mood swings, or who has had (or perhaps sought!) an eventful, challenging life. (Conversely, a flat plain may mean uneventfulness, boredom, or mild depression, and a gently rolling landscape suggests an even temperament or a peaceful, pleasant time.)

None of the above: A bare desert with no "extras"—no sources of shade or water, nothing to lean on—is a sign of extreme self-reliance. Whether because you've had to or because you choose to, you go it alone: You don't expect or ask for help. (The severity of your independence is softened if your Ladder is leaning up against the Cube; then, it's "you and me against the world.")

❂
A WORD ON TIME OF DAY

"It's afternoon . . . of course! I'm fifty-five," said our wonderful Dutch translator, Aleid Swierenga. The time of day may indeed indicate time of life, but it can also be a way of portraying the mood and "color" of this time in your life. A passionate young Italian-Canadian saw his Cube silhouetted against a blood-red sunset. A mystical, philosophical Japanese martial artist saw his Cube—actually a pyramid—bathed in moonlight. Time of day (and, of course, the weather) is the "lighting" of your stage, and a powerful factor in creating its mood.

Now that the stage is set . . . lights up . . . enter the Cube!

PART TWO

SECRETS
OF THE
CUBE

CHAPTER 3

POSITIONING
THE CUBE

@

C ubes can come in an infinite gradation of sizes; they can be made of an almost unlimited variety of materials. But a solid with six square sides can only turn up in a handful of basic positions. Therefore, if the infinite variety of Cubes can be grouped into a finite system of human types—like the twelve signs of the zodiac, or the nine points on the Enneagram—the position of the Cube offers the most practical basis for such a system. But is it also the most profound? Is the Cube's position really that fundamental and revealing? Most of all, does each position of the Cube consistently match up with a distinct personality profile?

We were fascinated to discover that the answer is yes, and yes.

When we asked, "Is the cube sitting flat on the sand, or in some other position?" you knew the answer right away. Everyone does—a telltale sign of the importance of position. The first moment you see your Cube, you see *where* it is and how it is oriented to the earth and sky. About two thirds of the people we've cubed say, "Yes, it's sitting right on the sand." The other third say, with equal conviction, "No! It's floating," or "It's standing on one of its points," or one of a few other positions—we've identified seven (with some subtype variations). A cube is a cube is a cube, but notice how changing its position transforms its shape—set it on one point and it's a diamond, bury part of it in earth and it's a pyramid—as well as radically alters its weightiness, stability, and "stackability." It's the transformational magic of position that frees the simple, stubborn form of a cube to represent the full range of human personalities.

The wisdom of the Cube, remember, is that it's not a self-portrait in a vacuum, but a portrait of you-in-the-world. The primacy of position says that nothing about us is more basic than our style of relating to this world with its three great dimensions: the earth of practical reality, the underworld of mystery and ancestry, and the sky of dreams, ideas, and ideals. Are you (or is someone you seek to understand) most at home in one of these dimensions? Or caught in one, yet yearning or striving toward another? Each position of the Cube has its own strengths and vulnerabilities, and each of the seven types instinctively generates a different force field, a different configuration of love and work around itself in order to thrive.

As you read about the seven positions, you'll recognize the special difficulties and rewards of being—or being with—each type, the needs that must be accommodated, and the resources you can rely on. When you combine this information with the size, distance, and material of the Cube—your own, or that of a person who matters to you—you'll have a rich and telling character portrait. Even before the companion Ladder and Horse reveal your style of relating to others, you'll already know a lot about your way of being, stumbling, and succeeding in relationships and at work.

Before we start, we should tell you how we arrived at these seven types. We didn't begin with the possible positions of a cube and then try to imagine what personality traits each might symbolize. Rather, the correlations between position and personality emerged gradually, but finally forcefully, out of the evidence of hundreds of Cubes. At first, bedazzled by the uniqueness of each Cube, we were skeptical of the seeming patterns that cropped up among the Cubes of our loved ones, and we watched to see if they would turn out to be consistent or just coincidental. When it became clear that the patterns weren't going to go away, we began testing their interpretive validity on the Cubes of people we didn't know personally.

We were just beginning that process when we cubed country-music star Tim McGraw for our first book. His Cube was transparent, but internally divided into "a lot of different cubes and cubicles inside of cubicles"—a wonderful image for the way his songs reveal his inner complexity. We asked him if it was sitting flat on the sand.

"No," he said, "it's up in the air, kind of moving a little bit. Floating."

"That *may* mean you, uh, live in ideas or in the spiritual world, more than in the practical world," we ventured, very tentatively.

"Well, I know *that's* true," drawled McGraw. "I'm not practical at all. I couldn't tell you how to pay a phone bill!"

Many, many such confirmations have emboldened us to define the seven types (and their subtypes). They are based on our years of field observations of Cubes "in the wild," and on our efforts (aided, in part, by the concept of the "three zones" in handwriting analysis)[1] to understand *why* the psyche chooses a particular position to symbolize a particular stance in life. We haven't yet conducted a scientific study, like that of French researcher Michel Gauquelin, whose statistical analysis discovered, for instance, that top athletes and military leaders were 5 percent likelier than other people to have a strong Mars in their astrological charts, while writers had a special relationship with the Moon, politicians with Jupiter, and scientists with Saturn. Maybe such a study will result from this book. We are confident that the significance of the seven positions will be confirmed.

Remember, though, that *you* are the final authority on your own Cube. If you don't think you are the type corresponding to the position of your Cube, or if that position holds a different, private meaning for you, first consider whether you're receiving and resisting new information about yourself that could make your self-image more objective and accurate. Ask the people who know you best. If you're still sure our interpretation doesn't

[1] *In* Personality in Handwriting *(Stephen Daye Press, 1947), Alfred O. Mendel explained the "zone doctrine" first formulated by Swiss graphologist Max Pulver in 1930 and still accepted by handwriting analysts today: "The upper 'third' of [a subject's] script is located in the intellectual, the conscious, sphere; his script therefore shows in the upper zone what he thinks and how he thinks, what he strives for, whether or not he has imagination, his pride and his ethical ideal." In a Cube landscape, sky and air are the "upper zone" of intellect, imagination, and ideals. The "lower zone," below the line on which a person writes—where letters like 'g' and 'y' have their "tails"—"harbors manifestations of things which are not even known to the writer himself. There we see what fills his unconscious, particularly the unconscious motives of his conscious activities and urges [Emotions, Instinct, Intuition, Drives]." This corresponds to the "underground" of your desert. "In the middle zone, where these two spheres meet, the writer's daily routine is portrayed, his social behavior and relations, his preferences and what he rejects." A Cube that's sitting on the sand occupies this "middle zone" of practical, everyday reality.*

fit—go with your own. Or if only parts of ours fit, use them to help you discover your own variation. As you now know, our own private symbol language sometimes departs from the common language.

THE SEVEN KEY POSITIONS

THE REALIST

THE VISIONARY

THE PRINCIPLED

■ THE PERFECTIONIST ■

■ THE EXPATRIATE ■

■ THE UNSUNG HERO ■

■ THE RECEPTIVE ■

CAN THE CUBE
CHANGE POSITION?

"But you can only play this game once!" protested a freshly cubed friend, indignant that its first, revelatory surprise could never quite be relived. (He hadn't yet discovered the endless fun of cubing his friends, his boss, his kids . . .) He's right, you can't "play it again, Sam"—at least not with the same innocence. But supposing you *could* play it again in a month, or a year, or five years, or twenty-five—would your Cube necessarily be in the same position? Are you a Realist or an Unsung Hero for life, the way you're a Scorpio or an Aries? Or could a major life change—coming from within or without—pick you up and put you down at a whole new angle? For that matter, if you could watch it, might you *see* your Cube changing its position in response to different moods or daily circumstances, the way people's personalities are said to advance or retreat to another point on the Enneagram when they're feeling safe or stressed? And finally, without being able to "play it again," how can we even answer these questions?

That a Cube *can*, in principle, change position is proven by the existence of type 5, the Expatriate. Clearly, no one starts out as an Expatriate. If that same person had been cubed back on his or her home ground, the Cube would not have been balancing on its edge. That precarious position reflects the psychic impact of a life-changing event: emigration. That makes it conceivable that other events of comparable import and impact could also reorient the Cube. It's possible at least to imagine a sadder-but-wiser Visionary, or a recovering addict, "coming down" to earth; an Unsung Hero pushed out into the limelight by erupting ambitions; a Perfectionist relaxing into a less driven position after therapy.

What's more, we've discovered that you *can* actually watch your Cube change. It's a living, breathing image, and if you check in with it every once in a while—just give it a glance in your mind's eye—you may see that something is different. Annie, for instance, entering a period of intense work, saw her Visionary Cube come down to earth with a thump and then get up on its point and start twirling—suggesting that while a dreamer first and foremost, she can go into Realist or Perfectionist mode if it's called for. Slobodan's humongous Realist Cube hasn't changed position, but it did change *shape,* morphing into a high black wall at a time when he faced some (partly self-created) obstacles in his profession. Jacques' titanium Cube has a change of position built in: At any moment, the SR-71 Blackbird can take off and whisk him from his streetwise realism into the Visionary stratosphere.

Astrologers say that the entire zodiac, with the potentials of all twelve signs, is present in every person's psyche; the sign you "are" is more accurately described as the sign that's *emphasized* by the pointer of the Sun. Similarly, you could say that all seven positions are potential in every Cube, and that in the right circumstances you could be—indeed, you probably *are*—sometimes a Perfectionist, sometimes a Visionary. . . . So as you read the seven types, you may see a little bit of yourself in each of them. And if you'd like to broaden your point of view, empathize with someone very different from you, or, for instance, leaven your realism with a little more vision, as you read each type, imagine repositioning *your* Cube. Levitate it. Or ground it. Bury it in the sand with one point sticking out. Balance it on a corner, or an edge. Imagine it as a space instead of a solid. It's as interesting to see which positions you resist as which ones feel most natural to you.

☺

CUBE MOBILITY

It's uncommon, but not unheard of, to see your Cube in motion. Occasionally a Cube will go tumbling along the ground, like a rolling stone; a Cube poised on one point, or floating in the air, may turn slowly—or spin frenetically. While too rare to define types of their own, these styles of movement seem to have quite consistent—and commonsense—meanings. (If these don't fit, imagine that you *are* your Cube, and see what free associations spin off from the sensation of turning or tumbling.)

■

Spinning usually signifies intense *busyness* (though it could also signal confusion, as in "my head is spinning"). This Cube generally belongs to the sort of person with lots of nervous energy, two cell phones, half a dozen deals or projects in the works, a daily class at the gym, three kids, and a dog. The busyness is usually productive and impressive; sometimes it's a bit intimidating. It can serve to keep others at a distance, to avoid both intimacy and introspection.

Turning is statelier and more deliberate. If this is your Cube, you may have several different "sides"—interests, opinions, moods—that you like to enjoy, or display, in alternation. You may have more than one "set" of friends. You may get bored with too much sameness, or identify with the sentiment, "Consistency is the hobgoblin of small minds." Indecision is also a possibility.

Tumbling naturally suggests rootlessness, questing, and perhaps noncommitment. You may be an adventurer, an explorer, a nomad, a wanderer—or just not ready to settle down and gather moss yet. There's also a lightheartedness and playfulness to this Cube, like a skipping child or a romping puppy—unless the Cube only tumbles when driven by the Storm. Then it signifies loss of control, being buffeted and even "blown away" by your troubles.

◉

CUBE COMPATIBILITY

Cubes, like the people they portray, differ in so many dimensions—not just position, but size, material, color, weight, hollowness or solidity, stillness or mobility—that there's no way to chart all possible combinations in love and work. Just as each Cube is unique, each relationship between two Cubes is unique. Still, our experience in cubing couples, friends, and coworkers shows that it *is* possible to predict how two Cubes in different positions—a Realist and a Visionary, for instance—will both complement and confound each other. Often a Realist is drawn to a Visionary for the imagination and inspiration the Visionary can provide, only to be exasperated by the Visionary's impracticality and mystified by the Visionary's penchant for living in fantasy. The Visionary, in turn, desperately needs the Realist's grounding and worldliness, but can find the Realist disappointingly unimaginative or materialistic.

The rule governing such attractions between unlikes, and even opposites, seems to be the one The Rolling Stones made famous in the song, "You Can't Always Get What You Want." The Visionary in love, for example, *wants* his or her fantasy lover but *needs* a real one. The surprise is that the work of self-knowledge in which the Cube is such a crafty tool is advanced by frustration at least as much as by fulfillment, for what we need most of all is insight into our own natures. The answer for a Visionary is *not* to stop being a Visionary and settle for straight reality, nor to go on being an ignorant Visionary and keep trying to find fantasy in reality, but to understand and accept that a Visionary needs both, each in its place.

For each of the seven positions, we've described its most characteristic attractions to, and misunderstandings with, partners in other positions. The Cube both provides an anatomy of the human comedy of relationships and helps us to learn its lessons rather than keep on repeating the same mistakes.

CHAPTER 4

THE
REALIST

KEY WORDS:

PRACTICALITY

COMPETENCE

VERSATILITY

PITFALLS:

LITERAL-MINDEDNESS

COMPLACENCY

CYNICISM

S itting on the sand is the most common position for the Cube. About two thirds of you will see your Cube in this position or one of its variations (slightly tilted; dug in; partly buried; face front; edge front). It's not surprising that this placement is the statistical norm: If a majority of us weren't down-to-earth—firmly in touch with practical, material reality—the human species would have died out long ago. On the other hand, if we were *all* down-to-earth, all the time, our yearning drive for innovation, betterment, and transcendence might have died out long ago.

Those of you whose Cubes are on the ground are tremendously diverse. A huge sandstone Cube, a tiny ice Cube, a waist-high plastic Cube, and a faceted gem of many-colored glass would seem, on the face of it, to have almost nothing in common. Nor can we claim that imagination and creativity are lacking among Realists. Grounded Cubes can be leavened by the sky element of inspiration in any number of ways, from reflecting clouds to incorporating rainbows to getting struck by lightning. They'll sometimes be linked to the heavens by their Ladders, signifying inspiration drawn from companions, colleagues . . . or a Friend Up There. And if your Cube is seen partially against the sky—its background bisected by the horizon line, the border between zones—you may be said to have "feet on the ground but head in the clouds," an excellent balance of vision and practicality. Read the description of the Visionary as well, for you will also have some of those characteristics.

Many accomplished artists, actors, and writers have down-to-earth Cubes—and that may be a key to their accomplishments. For what Realists share is not flat-footed literalism, but an acceptance, a mastery, even a relish for the world as it is.

◎

THE REALIST IN THE WORLD

Realists are competent and capable, fully engaged in this world with all its imperfections. They may sometimes deplore the way things are, but they never secede—quarreling with the world is a contact sport for a

Realist, another facet of involvement. And he or she is quick to call a truce when there's pleasure to savor or a living to be made. Realists don't feel they are too good for this world, and they don't fear being dirtied or compromised by it. The material, earth element—whether it's the body, money, or the hands-on stuff of work—is comfortable for them to deal with. The foursquare, stackable shape of the Cube in this position also suggests a basic comfort with *social* reality—getting along, belonging, fitting in—though extreme size or spatial isolation of the Cube may qualify this.

Realists are not escapists. Whatever personal problems or disappointments they encounter, they continue to take care of business—working, supporting their families, paying their bills (or deftly juggling their debts). Whatever system they find themselves in, they figure out how to work it. They are successfully reconciled with what Freud called the reality principle—the acceptance of things as they are in order to make them somewhat more as we wish. This makes for capable, productive workers and steady providers. Realists man the world, master it, and (as artists or leaders) faithfully reflect it, but without a powerful infusion of sky, they are unlikely to transform it.

That said, we happen to know four genuine world-changers with grounded Cubes—three successful writers (one of whom, Katherine Neville, used to be a banker) and a futurist/inventor (who also runs his late father's real-estate business). All four have uncannily similar Cubes. Three are variations on the transforming black slab in the film *2001*, and one, Neville's, is the Kaaba, the cubic black shrine in Mecca, which is said to house a meteorite. Each is a form that is firmly down to earth, but *came* from outer space.

THE REALIST AT WORK

Competence, productivity, thoroughness, responsibility, total absorption at work, yet also the ability to stop working and play, are characteristic of Realists in all walks of life (at least, until the Storm comes along). Realists are hard workers, but they work with more zest and matter-of-factness than compulsion or anxiety. They tend to have a high level of job satisfaction, or at least contentment, because their good grasp of the material and social world, concern for financial security, steady work habits, and realistic assessment of their own abilities enable them either to make the most of what work is available, or, if they are ambitious (as their Cube's size and material will show), to achieve what they envision. Cube a person with grand dreams who's stuck in a dead-end job—you'll rarely see a Cube on the ground. Realists either don't indulge in grand dreams, or if they have them, they're living them! Looking back, they'll be able to say, with the great jazzman Louis Armstrong, "I didn't wish for anything I couldn't get, and I got pretty near everything I wanted because I worked for it."

If you are a Realist, there's a good chance you found (or are still finding) your way to a good occupational fit by knocking around through a variety of jobs, having adventures, and picking up skills along the way. Realists tend to be led to their life's work by the winding ways of life itself, rather than being driven to it by a single, burning sense of mission. Many Realists are multitalented and multiskilled; quite a few have latent creative gifts, and, after some youthful artistic dabbling, settle for indirect expression in fields like construction, engineering, editing, entrepreneurship, law, talent management, or marketing. It's as if the Realist, like a cube flat on the ground, is well-balanced, well-rounded, level-headed, with no one particular faculty uppermost in the psyche and dominating it.

There are Realist thinkers and artists, of course. But when a Realist comes up with a world-class idea, it's usually one distilled from close scrutiny of some aspect of the world. Realists are keen observers and insightful analysts, not abstract theorists. (Freud and Darwin were probably Realists; Einstein almost certainly was not.) A Realist artist may play with the pure texture of paint, make sculpture from found objects, write lifelike fiction or political satire, take pictures, make movies or act in them, but it's always a collaboration with the world "out there." (Just a guess: Charles Dickens was a Realist; Emily Dickinson was not.) Like other Realists, Realist artists will achieve success if that is especially important to them, but it may not be—and they'll be just as productive for the sake of private satisfaction and a small audience, earning their living some other way. Being blocked is not a Realist's problem. Ambition is proportionate to ability, standards are not hopelessly high, materials are pliant and unintimidating, and ideas flow readily into form.

In a corporate setting, a Realist—whether executive or employee—can be relied on to stay informed, to assess situations factually rather than wishfully, to set sensible targets and meet deadlines, and to keep careful track of expenses. (Whether the Realist in question is better suited to *be* an executive or an employee—or his or her own boss—will be revealed by the relative size and position of the Cube and Ladder.) You definitely want a Realist, and not a Visionary, managing your finances. Realists are great at strategizing and implementing, putting ideas into action, but (depending on the material of the Realist's Cube) inspiration and innovation may have to come from more Visionary mentors, colleagues, or clients—a Ladder to the clouds. Reform, too, may depend on agitation by Principled colleagues; some Realists can be *too* accepting of the status quo, including its ever-present injustice and corruption. (Washington, D.C., must be full of them.) They'll go along to get along, or they'll bellyache but not take action.

Two things can drive a Realist crazy: having nothing to do, and having too much to do. On the one hand, as a Realist you *must* be productively engaged in the world. That's oxygen for you. Being sidelined or downsized can't stop you for long; you *will* find work to do. Worse, especially for a young Realist, is being undecided among too many options. With multiple talents but no one strong calling, you can become immobilized, and you will suffer. Then, you may allow the need for money, or another person, or a random opportunity to sweep you back into the stream of life and set a course for you. That's fine: Some of the best Realist careers have begun by chance.

At the other extreme, millions of Realists are suffering from the enforced hyperactivity of the computer-fax-cell-phone-pager age. Realists are willing workers, but not natural-born workaholics. They like, and are good at, a balance of work and family, work and play. They're quite capable of "turning it off" and going home at five o'clock. But they're also help-lessly attuned to the zeitgeist *and* conscientious about getting all their work done. So they're swept along by the accelerating culture, hating every frazzled minute of it. Realists are the majority; if *they* went out on strike, they could probably put the brakes on our runaway culture. Alas, Realists are also the most prone to say, "What can I do? That's the world we live in."

☞

THE REALIST IN LOVE

You'll need to consult the Ladder, Horse, and Flowers for a full reading of your (or your loved one's) emotional "force field"—the unique spatial array of relationships that reveals a soul's push and pull, the way iron filings make the field of a magnet visible. However, there are a few basic traits common to most Realists that can lay a foundation for your understanding.

Realists in love seem to go to one of two extremes. Often they are clear-eyed and sensible about it, choosing partners for all the right reasons, not rushing into foolish liaisons, and establishing bonds strong on affection, common interests, and companionship (as well as sex). But for some, love is the one place where the irrational erupts into their lives. Outbreaks of obsession and jealousy (their own or others') can disrupt their otherwise practical existence so badly that they end up going cold turkey, keeping their balance by dividing love into platonic friendships and brief sexual encounters. Even neurotic Realists prefer self-preservation to agony and ecstasy and would rather be alone than crazy. A happier reconciliation of opposites occurs when an earthbound Realist lets magic into his or her life by falling for someone who has a floating Cube and/or is pictured as a winged horse or a unicorn.

Realists are responsible about money and will never let their loved ones starve. After (and sometimes before) their own security, the main reason they insist on being gainfully employed is so they can take good care of those they care for. (On the other hand, they can also be protective of their personal assets, the kind of person who insists on a prenuptial agreement.) A Realist who is financially insecure may refrain from getting involved.

If you are happily involved with a Realist, he or she will never be a deadbeat, will always make a strong contribution to joint finances (by managing money if not making it), may even be the sole provider, and will make sure there is insurance in case anything happens to him or her. In addition, Realists are famously handy, so they'll bring all sorts of valuable skills to a household, from cooking to carpentry. It's a holdover from traditional gender roles that Realist women so often manage to fall in love with responsible men, while Realist men sometimes delight in supporting a less practical woman. But more and more Realist women insist on their own earning power, and in today's economy, more and more men are finding that an asset.

REALIST SEX

Realists are usually at home in their bodies and have healthy appetites for food and other pleasures of the senses (including music, art, and nice furnishings), as well as sex. Being creatures of the flesh isn't a problem for them, though as creatures of their time and place, they may dutifully fight weight—and lose (the fight, not the weight). But Realists don't struggle for self-control the way Perfectionists do. They either indulge in moderation, reconcile themselves to their vices (and the consequences), or make a rational decision and quit.

Such sexual hang-ups as a Realist may have are really emotional. Avoidance of closeness or dependency, for instance, may show up as spatial isolation of the Cube, or inability to see a Horse. The problem, then, is not between the Realist and his or her own sexuality, but between the Realist and other people. But even a commitment-phobic Realist will rarely withdraw into celibacy. Most Realists enjoy the life of the body and don't make a big deal of it. Sex is just a welcome, proportionate part of life. (This can be frustrating for a Visionary partner who *does* want to make a big romantic deal of it, or for a moody, hypersensitive Perfectionist. Realists can be quite meat-and-potatoes about sex—direct in their appetites, but then on to something else.)

❧

THE REALIST AT PLAY

Realists play just as hard—and as noncompulsively—as they work. They are active people, full of fearless curiosity about the world, who find it more fun and relaxing to *do* something than to space out in front of the TV and dream. They like to go out to restaurants, parties, and cultural events. Their competence is versatile, and they've often mastered—at enjoyable amateur levels—several sports, hobbies, games, and/or crafts. And they're often interested in learning new ones. One male Realist friend of ours, in his forties, is now taking both flying and cooking lessons, and recently got certified as a scuba diver. Another friend, a woman in her eighties, keeps busy cleaning and repairing her house, cooking delicious meals for family holidays, keeping up correspondence with friends in several countries, reading and clipping magazines, and sorting through family papers.

Realists relax in motion. Being a beginner or a competitor doesn't make them anxious, because they trust their basic competence and don't expect the impossible of themselves—unlike Perfectionists. A Realist partner will constantly be trying, against strong resistance, to get a Perfectionist to loosen up and a Visionary (who likes to read and daydream) to come out of his or her shell. As we'll see, this holds possibilities for both conflict and complementarity. Only when you truly understand how you differ can you be a breath of fresh air to your partner, not a nag and a reproach.

REALIST SUBTYPES

■ THE QUIET REBEL ■

subtle nonconformity
subversive humor
whimsy

When someone makes a point of describing the Cube as slightly tilted, she or he takes pride in a subtle but significant departure from the norm. Without making a fuss, this person just won't quite be a four-square building block of society, and inwardly goes his or her own way. Look for independence of opinion, mild eccentricity, enjoyment of one's own foibles, subversive or whimsical humor.

The Realist

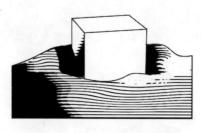

- STAND MY GROUND -

rooted
stubborn
opinionated
loyal

People with a dug-in Cube have a strong sense of who they are and where they stand. This position can signify strong roots in one's family or ethnic background or present home place. It can also point to bulldog stubbornness, an unwillingness to budge once one has taken a position or a stand—the defiant attitude expressed in Tom Petty's song "I Won't Back Down." This can be a wonderful, courageous quality in a lover, friend, or coworker. It can also be quite exasperating.

This person may be slow to compromise, to admit being wrong, or to see another person's point of view. He or she may enjoy arguing. On the other hand, she or he is also intensely loyal, attached, and will spring to your defense.

▪ HIDING OUT ▪

unobtrusive
undercover
avoiding attention

A Cube partially buried in the sand—usually a small one—belongs to a person who seeks concealment, finds freedom in obscurity, prefers to "fly below the radar" of others' attention. There are different reasons for being in hiding; check the Cube's material and appearance for clues. An artist we know, an emigré from Eastern Europe, prefers to keep a low profile, not only for self-protection but because for her, invisibility equals freedom, including the freedom to observe and sketch people. (Her Cube is the color of the sand, so camouflaged you could easily overlook it and not know it was there.) Another woman's sharp-edged little black Cube, however, seemed to be lying spitefully in wait to ambush someone. If you overlooked *hers* and stepped on it, it would hurt your sole, but good! (She had a cat named Ouch!)

When it's the Storm that comes along and dumps sand on the Cube, the meaning can be quite different (see page 265).

■ THE PUBLIC FACE ■

controlled
compartmentalizes life
conceals emotion

In its most natural, relaxed position, a Cube on the ground would be showing part of two sides, like a person who's comfortable revealing different sides of herself or himself. Most Realists see their Cubes that way and don't even comment on it. Occasionally someone will make a point of saying two sides can be seen; such a person consciously enjoys having "different sides" and being known from different angles.

But when the Cube is carefully placed so that only one face is visible, it signals a desire to control how one is seen; to appear perfectly consistent; or to keep public and private selves separate. If this person describes the hidden sides at all, they are often of a different color or material. He or she has unusual self-control, public poise, and some difficulty with or dislike of showing emotion, except perhaps to a trusted few.

■ COMIN' AT YA ■

energetic   *active*
dynamic   *pioneering*

When the Cube is specifically described as edge front, two sides are visible, true—but that's not what's important. It's the aggressive energy of that edge, bearing down on you like the prow of a ship. The person is physically and mentally vital, fearless, enterprising, impatient, always on the go. He or she is a doer who breaks new ground, slices through red tape, cuts to the chase.

At work, this is a dynamo who can't be stopped. The job had better allow some room for physical movement, as well as financial or creative worlds to conquer. (Try sticking an ocean liner behind a desk!) In personal relationships, the sheer energy can knock you down and roll right over you, unless you can match it. This person can be exhausting (and sometimes cutting), but is tireless and great fun to do things with.

A friend of ours whose Cube looks like this is a tremendously active real-estate developer who literally comes bounding toward you with his coattails flying.

The Realist

CHAPTER 5

THE
VISIONARY

KEY WORDS:

DREAMER

ORIGINAL

INCURABLE ROMANTIC

PITFALLS:

IMPRACTICALITY

ABSENTMINDEDNESS

DISILLUSIONMENT

Quick, what's the opposite of down-to-earth? Is there a term that's not derogatory? We don't have a perfect word or phrase in English for the person represented by a floating Cube. But that word exists in Yiddish: *Luftmensh*.

"Air person" is the literal translation, but it doesn't mean "airhead," or "up in the air," nor yet "walking on air." Rather, this is someone who floats free above the housetops of sensible domestic life like the lovers, dreamers, scholars, and fiddlers painted by Chagall. This person's home base isn't on earth, in consensus reality and common sense, but in the more beautiful world of intellect, spirit, or imagination. Ideas, dreams, or visions are more real to him or her than the grocery list, the evening news, even the rent—a quality linking people otherwise as different as brilliant scientists and visionary artists, messianic leaders and mountain hermits, drug and alcohol addicts (yes, this Cube is "high") and incurable dreamers, the Walter Mittys of this world.

A Visionary's degree of otherworldliness is directly proportionate to his or her Cube's distance from the ground; the far ends of that range (hovering inches above the sand; way out in the stratosphere) are different enough to define distinct subtypes. But the majority of Visionaries maintain some kind of tie to the earth plane, however tenuous and ambivalent. Maybe the horizon line passes behind the Cube so that part of it is at least seen against an earthy background. (That's Annie's situation, and she does love the *idea* of being practical. She just hasn't gotten around to it yet.) Often it's the Ladder that anchors the Cube to the ground, or an earthbound Horse whose attraction is stronger than gravity. Whatever it is, that tie is crucial to survival and fulfillment, for it's here on earth that a Visionary's visions must be realized, expressed, and shared—or stay locked in his or her head. All too often, they do.

֍

THE VISIONARY IN THE WORLD

. . . Is out of this world. Is here under protest. Is disappointed with reality for not measuring up to the beauty of pure ideas, spiritual visions, political utopias, or romantic dreams. Visionaries have been hurt by the real world, often very early. This position is chosen at the moment when a hurt or rejected child discovers the dazzling consolations of the imagination. Most Visionaries felt like outsiders when they were young. But did they retreat into their dreams because others treated them like outsiders . . . or did they get treated that way because they were already dreamy and different? Which came first, the strange bird or the egg?

Visionaries serve a vital function for the rest of us. We humans come equipped with the puzzling, often painful ability to imagine a world much lovelier than the one we have to live in, and it's Visionaries who do most of the imagining. In the process, they either fire up the rest of us—with hope, idealism, escapism, solace, or zeal—or they are heartbroken and frustrated all over again by the stubborn sordidness of reality. But they are rarely crushed by it: Visionaries have a weird resiliency, protected by their ability to withdraw into a world of their own. Once there, they may ignore the "real" world or nurse a grudge against it. The alleged Unabomber started out as a pure mathematician—as Visionary as it gets—and ended up hurling his mail bombs down like lightning bolts on what he saw as a gross and indifferent world.

Visit a Visionary's home, and you'll either find a bewitching nest or a disorder and dilapidation no Realist or Perfectionist would tolerate for a minute. And somewhere in the clutter is a bunch of unpaid bills. The Visionary simply tunes it all out, content with the riches of the spirit—or convinced that this week will bring a winning lottery ticket. As Hamlet put it, "I eat th'air, promise-crammed."

Visionaries are often indifferent to the making and management of money, casually grand about giving it away, and susceptible to the lure of sweepstakes, casinos, pyramid schemes, and high-risk investments. That's because a Visionary's only reason for wanting money is to be free of it. The freedom hard-won by carefully managing it requires too much attention to something that, for a Visionary, isn't interesting or even real. Money comes alive only as cosmic caprice and spite, that force that seems to delight in frustrating Visionaries. (If you are one, you know what we mean.) If we could, the world's Visionaries would join hands and wish money away. Yet for a charmed few, dreams make millions to make more dreams. Do you think three Realists founded DreamWorks SKG?

Other aspects of the material world—computers, carpentry, plumbing, cooking, cars, housework, and the like—are more neutral, having the potential to be either friend or foe. Many Visionaries view such things with bafflement or indifference, as being outside the real world of the mind or stumbling blocks or rude intrusions in it. But if a Visionary becomes convinced that some material thing or skill can help create or protect his or her dream world, that slice of the outside world becomes intimate and hyperreal, as if a spotlight hit it. The Visionary will zero in on it and master it with the ravenous thoroughness of fire consuming tinder, whether it's a scientist's lab apparatus, a singer-songwriter's guitar, a romance novelist's word processor, or a misanthrope's mountain cabin. One Visionary we know, actually the far-out Eccentric subtype, acquired a sailboat and taught himself to sail and maintain it; it's like his Cube, his own little planet. Annie feels that way about her car, which she drives very well, and which, with the radio going, is no material machine to her, but a transport of emotion.

THE VISIONARY AT WORK

Visionaries have wonderful ideas. Whether those ideas ever see the light of day, whether they do the Visionary or anyone else any earthly good, depends on establishing at least diplomatic relations with the earth plane, and preferably a working alliance. The biggest hurdle for a Visionary is *manifestation*—getting those visions into words or material form. Too much can seem lost in translation, the way dreams fade on waking; Visionaries are easily discouraged by the necessary struggles with resistant matter and human obtuseness or indifference—the very struggles combative Realists relish. It's so effortless and fulfilling just to "Imagine" (à la John Lennon), to pull up the spaceship's ramp, close the hatch, and live in your head. The Visionary who yields to that temptation makes one absentminded employee. She or he needs either 1) an utterly routine job, which will provide the necessities but require little attention (suspect your mail carrier); 2) a trust fund; or 3) a Realist partner who will support, protect, and honor the dreamer for the ever-present reminder that we don't live by bread alone. Visionaries can be contented housewives or househusbands, since daydreams and dish suds go together quite nicely.

Other Visionary entrepreneurs, inventors, and artists engage in repeated, tragicomic struggles to bring ideas into the world. The Small

Business Administration, the U.S. Patent Office, Hollywood, and Broadway are mute witnesses to the launching, and often the sinking, of thousands of hopeful, homemade ships. There's something quixotic and heroic about the indefatigability of these Visionaries. Their brainstorms may be less than obvious to the rest of us (but that can be *our* fault), their presentation skills may be less than polished, but their imagination is irrepressibly fertile, and their optimism springs eternal: *They* see so clearly why the world needs *this* idea or gizmo or Azerbaijan restaurant, this time their conviction will surely be infectious! And sometimes it is. Odds are Sylvester Stallone was a Visionary back when he wouldn't give up on his rejection-tattered screenplay, *Rocky.* (Success may or may not have brought his Cube down to earth.) We'll never know for sure about Jonathan Larson, the late author of the musical *Rent,* but we can guess.

If you know you are a Visionary—and it usually shows up in a day-dreamy childhood—there are three things you can acquire (things a parent or mentor should have nagged you to acquire) that will make your life immeasurably easier and more fulfilling: a niche, a skill, and/or a practical partner.

There are niches for Visionaries. Academia is one, a refuge where pure thinkers and artists in residence are provided with offices, labs, reams of blank time, and captive audiences. It's a shrinking niche, but it still exists. The catch is, true Visionaries are at odds with institutions and orthodoxies. Especially in conservative fields like science, they may have to rein in their originality for years (if they can) to establish their credentials. The New Age world of workshops and holistic therapies, on the other hand, is a growing niche that's very hospitable to Visionaries. (In fact, its very availability may be breeding more Visionaries, like mushrooms.) Think tanks might be another possibility. And need we mention computer wizardry?

The kinds of skills Visionaries are well advised to acquire are expressive skills. Become a good writer, speaker, artist, musician, architect, and you will succeed in sharing your inner visions with the world—and earning your living at it. Contrary to Visionary belief, becoming good at such things is less a matter of "talent" than of dogged work. Visionaries as a group probably have more raw talent, and achieve less, than Realists. It's not that Visionaries are particularly lazy. They're just so good at imagining that they want to give up in despair when their unskilled fingers make mush of their minds' conceptions. The greatest harm is done to young Visionaries when no one shows them how hard aspiring artists have to work—and that it pays off. They need the experience of training and persevering until suddenly some bit of the original vision shines forth in sound or words or stone. Then they're hooked.

"A practical partner" can be a life partner, a business partner, or—in a corporate context—the facilitating staff that bustles a Visionary's ideas away like a queen bee's eggs and nurtures them to fruition. It's quite common for a floating Cube to be connected to the ground by the Ladder, and this shows the Visionary's awareness of being symbiotically dependent on one or more Realists for grounding, materialization of ideas, and a steady supply of sandwiches and paper clips. (At least one of the three partners in Dream-Works SKG—Steven Spielberg, Jeffrey Katzenberg, or David Geffen—is bound to be a Realist.) The scientist designs experiments to test her theories; graduate students carry them out. The architect drafts his dream building; engineers make it stand up. The artist creates the work; an agent makes the deals. These are ideal setups for Visionaries, and should be a model for their role in the business world.

Visionaries make inspiring leaders and inspired brainstormers, excelling in fields like advertising and product development. But their ideas often need to be brought down to earth, translated into what's possible. And beware the Visionary who won't delegate the details. The inspired CEO or manager who insists things be done *exactly* as she or he envisions can drive a company, or at least its employees, into the ground. Number-crunching and reality-testing just aren't this person's strong suits. If chaos is to be averted, others must be trusted to test-drive the ideas and write the budgets.

There are rare Visionaries who connect with the earth plane solely through the emanations of their powerful personalities. These people can project their visions directly to other minds and change things on earth—for better or worse—by the sheer force of charisma and will. They are spellbinders, saints and stars and dictators, and they have the power to draw us all into their dream or nightmare worlds. (In what other category could you find both Marilyn Monroe and Adolf Hitler?) It isn't easy either to be them or to be around them, but it is electrifying. Compared to other periods in history, there seems to be a shortage of that kind of Visionary right now. Perhaps their power is activated by extremes of lonely hardship that affluence, peace, and psychotherapy have made more rare. Thank God—or should we say, too bad?

THE VISIONARY IN LOVE

Most Visionaries are romantics. (Even the cerebral Visionary, who lives in the intellect, usually hides romantic yearnings.) Love is right up their alley, and they can become its addicts, because love in its early stages is the most convincing enchantment we know. The whole world is transfigured; we're like Dorothy stepping into full-color Oz. The brain chemistry of infatuation puts us in a drugged trance where we believe *the dream has actually come true*—and that's the state Visionaries want to live in all the time!

Not that Visionaries have a monopoly on idealizing fantasy; we mentioned those Realists who fall for flying unicorns. But Realists will try to have a real, share-the-toothbrush relationship even with a unicorn, while Visionaries specialize in fantasy relationships. Unrequited love actually suits them, because the imagined bliss of the lost or longed-for love is never shattered by getting it. Should the beloved suddenly turn and requite, or the married lover actually file for divorce, the Visionary might well flee in confusion, instinctively protecting his or her vow of fidelity to the dream. Visionary women tend to find nice, plain, devoted men unexciting; they're holding out for devotion *plus* thrills (probably a contradiction in terms). Visionary men are often commitment-phobic, keeping themselves free for the "magic lady" who never quite materializes.

In spite of this, Visionaries can eventually make good marriages, and need to. Rarely, two Visionaries will fuse in a beatific or pyrotechnic *folie à deux.* Or the Visionary, after holding out for years or divorcing more than once, finally finds someone magical enough to adore (for the older Visionary man, it's almost inevitably someone twenty or thirty years his junior). More commonly, an earthbound partner will offer anchorage and protection. Once a Visionary grudgingly acknowledges the need for those things, he or she will suffer to be bound—but with a sense of compromise or concession, holding something in reserve. In many, if not most, relationships, one person is more the lover, the other more beloved. The Visionary will often be the latter, justifying the descent into mere reality by saying "He (she) needs me," rather than admitting the truth that "I need him (her)." Or, having accepted an earthly partner, the Visionary will do an imaginative makeover, digging up and burnishing the person's modest virtues till they gleam with heroism.

A Japanese friend of ours, well into her thirties, has a floating canary-yellow Cube and an abiding crush on an American rock star, whom she met once. Only when her attempts to reconnect with the rock star failed decisively did she agree to marry a plain, stolid suitor twenty years her senior. She has embroidered this man's very plainness and stolidity into rare and wondrous human qualities—and when he smiles at her radiantly, he doesn't look so plain. He is her rock, but she still loves the rock star, too. Two Horses, one brown, one white, are tethered below her Cube.

This is a classic Visionary happy ending. Secret allegiance to the dream—in the form of an unforgotten first love, a celebrity crush, a work-place flirtation, a romance novel a week—makes it okay for the Visionary to be in a real relationship. This way, you can have your cake and eat bread, too. The ending is less happy when the Visionary keeps trying to make the dream come true. Quite a few are prone to affairs or serial monogamy as they chase the fleeting dream through a succession of real bodies. It's a wise and mature Visionary who knows that the ideal lover really exists—in the imagination—and must stay there, or die like a fish out of water.

VISIONARY SEX

If sex for a Realist is meat and potatoes (or at least a big plate of pasta), sex for a Visionary is ambrosia—not a frank carnal pleasure but a soulful, spiritual rush. Even a Visionary philanderer is after more than just the physical act; there has to be fusion or danger, some sense of "swept away," and the lover has to haunt or ignite the imagination, not just the hormones. Sensation and yearning are more important than orgasm, and crucial to its intensity as an event in the psyche, not the genitalia. A Visionary's favorite part of lovemaking may be something more subtle, a first caress or the moment of penetration. Fleetwood Mac's "Seven Wonders" could be the Visionary anthem—an entire song celebrating this momentous event: "You touched my hand." Some Visionaries may use fantasy and role-playing to raise the stakes and the emotional voltage of sex. Straightforward pornography, however, revolts them. Female Visionaries would rather not be reminded that such sublime music is made on such absurd organs. Male Visionaries may share other men's fascination with body parts, but prefer to view them through a poetic eye.

In a long-term relationship, especially with a Realist, a Visionary's non-physical needs may not be satisfied unless she or he can spike lovemaking with fantasy—private or shared. The hurt partner who asks, "What, I'm not enough for you?" needs to understand that sex—even the word, "sex"—lacks the mystical aura Visionaries feed on. Affection and honest lust *aren't* enough. They have to be seasoned with just a soupçon of Heathcliff. Of course, the tireless quest for intensity can become tiresome. It's a good sign when a Visionary learns how to laugh in bed.

❧

THE VISIONARY AT PLAY

Visionaries are escape artists, always searching for that magic exit to another world. They love Caribbean vacations, and big fat beach novels, and operas (soap and grand), and their own daydreams (and night dreams). Unlike Realists, who always like to be busy trying something new, Visionaries may look idle and unsociable during their downtime. But they are just extremely self-sufficient. They don't need many, or any, toys from the outside. Their inner world is swarming with action, emotion, and invention, just they way they like it.

But go to a good dramatic movie with a Visionary, and you'll both be wrapped in its atmosphere for hours. If you want him or her to get out of that armchair and come play with you, go to Mardi Gras, or the nearest aquarium or planetarium, or historic Williamsburg, or one of those dinners where they stage a murder mystery. Go bird-watching. Even go to Disney World. The meeting ground for a Visionary and a more outer-worldly type is any activity that provokes the imagination and involves an element of "What if?" or "Let's pretend." The Realist goes scuba diving for the fun and challenge, the Visionary because it's so different and dreamlike down there. The Realist aspires to be a seasoned scuba diver, while the Visionary wonders what it's like to be a moray eel. In that way, Visionaries are child-like. They are never happier, at work or play, than when they can see the outside world as enchanted and so can live, undivided, in the dream.

❧

VISIONARY SUBTYPES

▪ THE INTUITIVE ▪

accurate hunches
impulsive
keeping options open

A person whose Cube hovers inches to a few feet above the sand is almost—but not quite—a Realist. He or she stays close to the facts, yet is open to hunches and surprises, navigating through the real world by intuition. The little gap between the Cube and the ground, like the gaps in an intuitive person's handwriting, signifies the leaps of association that can lead an Intuitive to a correct conclusion by a nonlogical route. The blend of realism and inspired insight can make this person lucky and successful in a way that mystifies others.

However, he or she can also be a bit unpredictable. Like a hovercraft that can suddenly dart off in an unexpected direction, the Intuitive may impulsively quit a job, start a new project, or agree to go on an impromptu trip. There is a relish for the non sequitur, the incongruous, and the unexpected. Indecision, lack of commitment, reluctance to settle down, or a sense of too many possibilities may also accompany this position.

■ THE ECCENTRIC ■

willful independence
a different drummer

You may need a telescope to see the Eccentric's Cube (well, not quite). It's out there in its own orbit, out of range of conventional obligation and influence, with only the remotest relationship to the earth plane. But that doesn't necessarily mean the Eccentric is a space cadet. What it does mean is extreme independence. This person is not much influenced by society and doesn't care about influencing it. He or she has escaped the gravitation of the collective and wants only to go his or her own way. Eccentrics will deal efficiently and pleasantly with society to the minimal extent necessary to secure autonomy and deflect interference. But outside opinion doesn't concern them emotionally.

Don't assume that the Eccentric is a nut. In a routinely mad world, true sanity may well appear eccentric. Eccentrics tend to be confident and serene. They have their own absorbing interests, which are pursued for their own sake, not for reward or recognition ("outsider art" is a good example). Some Eccentrics have a matter-of-fact personal faith: God understands them, so what if no one else does? Others are convinced atheists, classical Stoics. In either case, the Eccentric has an unshakable belief system that works for him or her.

Like the Little Prince, the Eccentric lives on his or her own little planet. Being in a relationship doesn't change that. Most Eccentrics have mastered the art of coexistence. When you visit their planet you're expected to play by their rules, but outside of that, you can have quite a life of your own. Eccentrics won't give you a lot of sympathy and understanding—they're too tuned in to their own different drummer to want to hear what makes you tick—but they will give you both companionship and freedom. It's a rare and undervalued combination.

CHAPTER 6

THE
PRINCIPLED

KEY WORDS:

IDEALS

ACTIVISM

INTEGRITY

PITFALLS:

SELF-RIGHTEOUSNESS

BURNOUT

I f your Cube is perched on a high place—a dune, hill, cliff, or rise—it's in touch with the earth, yet above the common plane. (If that high place is a pedestal, it's an intensifier: For your subtype, everything we're about to say is doubly true.) You will know what this "aboveness" means to you: a sense of superiority, perhaps, or a far-seeing perspective. For the majority of your cohorts we've cubed, though, it signifies high personal standards—ethical, moral, and professional. This Cube belongs to someone who lives firmly on earth, but is determined to make the earth a better place, or at least to live a principled life on it, even in the midst of cheerful corruption, compromise, and betrayal.

A Principled person is someone you can look up to—if also someone who may have a slight tendency to look down on you. Crusaders, reformers, whistle-blowers, the cop who's *not* on the take, the book editor who loves literature, the socially responsible CEO, the truly faithful spouse: They are beacons in the murk of a venal time, inspiring by their example and chastising by their undimmed outrage. Their defining characteristic is righteousness—in both the positive and the negative sense.

⊚

PRINCIPLED IN AN UNPRINCIPLED WORLD

This Cube's position reminds us of the determined heroine in a Western who arrives in a muddy little frontier town and lifts her skirts above the mire to march across the town's one so-called street and start reforming everyone in the tavern. Principled people do their best to hold themselves above the mire and above the fray—while staying in the middle of the action. They don't have the Visionary's willful innocence; they are worldly people, engaged in worldly pursuits, who know very well what kind of world they live in. But they don't shrug with sorrowful cynicism, like many Realists do; nor do they wish it were some other world, or withdraw into an imaginary one, like the Visionary. Rather, they fight to raise its standards by playing their own part impeccably and, when necessary, by challenging or rallying others.

Principled people tend to hold strong political convictions, whether on the right or the left. "Social justice" or "family values" aren't mere buzzwords to them, but urgently needed medicine for society's ills. And corruption is a scourge they will not tolerate, no matter how many weary Realists tell them that fighting it is like carrying a beach away grain by grain of sand. Both active and generous in supporting whatever causes they believe in, the Principled are citizens par excellence.

If your Cube is on a high place, you probably have a few, true friends you respect and who respect you; outside that small circle, you may be regarded with hostility, contempt, or disbelief, as well as admiration and relief. (You can take comfort from the fact that you are a vitally important influence on young people.) You must understand that for others, a Principled person is stirring, shaming, and sometimes inconvenient to be around. To encounter someone who actually lives by a code of honor can be an invigorating shock, like a blast of fresh winter air; it can also be a slap in the face if you've let your own honor sag or slide. Boy/girl scout, goody-goody, holier-than-thou, Mr. Clean—from the schoolyard to the boardroom, these are some of the taunts aimed at the Principled by those whom their mere presence puts on the defensive, or whose little schemes are hindered by Principled vigilance and incorruptibility.

Are Principled people too good to be true—and proud of it? They often place their Ladders—friends and colleagues—below the Cube's level, down on the ground or leaning against the dune or hill. Do they flaunt their moral superiority, turn up their clean noses at muddied mortals, get an ego kick from their integrity? Well . . . maybe a *little*. But if you're one of them, you know you earn it the hard way. You expect from others only what you already demand—and get—from yourself. Because you know a principled life is possible, your indignation at slackers is sincere. What others mostly resent is the reproach of your example. If you're *involved* with a Principled person, at home or at work, you know it's like coming face to face with your own conscience. You'll either be inspired to clean up your act, or you'll be seriously annoyed. Sometimes both.

☙

THE PRINCIPLED AT WORK

Highly principled people often—and willingly, if not happily—pay a price in career advancement for their unyielding integrity. If it comes to a choice between what's right and what's personally advantageous, they are constitutionally unable to "go for it." It's a safe bet that they were not well represented among the junk bond traders and corporate raiders of the eighties, nor would they likely have the requisite ruthlessness to downsize well in the nineties. Profit maximization *über alles* is not their kind of principle. They consistently put quality before quantity, ethics before strategy, loyalty before power.

That's not to say that the Principled don't care about success and effectiveness—but they insist on coming by it honestly, or not at all. In a word, they're old-fashioned. And they are often nostalgic for a more chivalrous time, when, say, publishing was a gentleman's business, and literature had not been eclipsed by the blockbuster; or when an important part of the pay-off for even the humblest job was pride in doing it well. If you are Principled, you probably continue to work that way even in our vastly accelerated, corner-cutting, win-at-any-price society. You take the time that is needed to do each task scrupulously. You champion projects that are not obviously commercial but that you believe in. You remain loyal to old associates who are deserving but unsuccessful. This makes you something of an anachronism, and it may limit your material prospects, but it satisfies your soul.

As an employee, you are both a priceless asset and a time bomb. Your employer can trust you utterly—unless *she* or *he* is crooked. Then, watch out! You understand whistle-blowers who sacrifice their jobs for the truth, and those rare lawyers who bankrupt themselves for a pro bono case. The more cynical type of Realist may scoff, "What a schmuck," but you prefer the clean, bittersweet taste of integrity to the canned whipped cream of quick success. You are happiest when self-employed as a craftsperson, small entrepreneur, or professional; working (or volunteering) as an activist with a nonprofit organization; or employed by a small, quality concern that balances modest, steady profit with excellence, values, and social responsibility. If you choose to take on "the system" in a large organization, industry, or government, more power to you, but be warned: The pitfalls are burnout, bitterness, and self-righteous martyrdom.

None of this is to say that there aren't Principled men and women in the Fortune 500 or on the best-seller lists. Persevering in one's principles isn't necessarily the road to genteel obscurity or noble ruin. It can be the high road to success. The Principled little guy, like the Eccentric, is sometimes "discovered" by a journalist or "outed" by a colleague who thinks his or her dogged consistency and stubborn integrity make a fascinating human-interest story. The result may be a Kiwanis award, a bonus and a raise, a "local hero" story, an item in *Time* or *People,* even a TV movie of the week. The Principled big shot, that rare public servant or businessperson who proves that hard work and morality are just as marketable as your soul, is the best antidote to post-Watergate cynicism, for his or her example will trickle down. Such men and women are the role models of responsible leadership that we so desperately need.

@

THE PRINCIPLED IN LOVE

The Principled person brings the same high standard of conduct to relationships as he or she does to work. Fidelity, honesty, and old-fashioned devotion combined with a modern respect for the other person's freedom all make love and marriage with a Principled partner nice work if you can get it. Cubes in this position are about as common as people who *really, truly* consider their marriage vows to be binding "for better or for worse, till death do us part."

Since we're talking about human beings and not Platonic solids, however, nothing's perfect. The heart can be a hot, unprincipled organ, and the only way to bring it under the just and rational rule of principle is to cool it down. Therefore, to the extent that Principled lovers succeed in loving by their principles, they may be—or may *appear* to be—lukewarm in their passions. But the hidden intensity of their feelings comes to light when they are hurt. And they do get hurt. Shy, gallant, and considerate, they may lose out in courtship to some dashing son of a bitch or his mother who sweeps their intended away. (Think of the sedate reverence with which Ingrid Bergman gazed at Paul Henreid—"Victor Laszlo"—in *Casablanca*. Now, think of how she looked at bad boy Bogie.) Or they may grant a partner so much trust and freedom that she or he simply walks off with someone else. Or they may get so obsessed with some occupational or political crusade that their marriage dies of neglect. (A Principled crusader who's single will often remain solitary, wedded to the cause.)

As worldly, wary, and tough as they can be in public life, the Principled revere hearth and home and remain astonishingly innocent about the devious ways of love. When a partner walks, the Principled lover is usually caught by surprise, and feels shocked, devastated, and betrayed. He or she had assumed that love was a done deal, that the other person was equally committed and took their bond just as cozily for granted. Some Principled jiltees blame themselves; others turn self-righteous and vindictive in divorce negotiations, especially when children are being wronged.

On the other hand, if it's the Principled partner who strays, he or she will feel shame, guilt, and confusion, literally torn between fixed principles and the runaway heart. The belief in honesty may compel this person to make a tactless confession that does more harm than good. She or he may either sacrifice a truly passionate love to stay married, or sacrifice heavily in the divorce settlement as a way of paying penance. Another, rather clever move is to make open marriage itself into a high principle, vowing lifelong fidelity to the heart's truth.

All that said, the fact remains that the Principled person makes a wonderful partner if you're sane or mature enough to value integrity, thoughtfulness, and commitment. He or she is someone you can admire, trust, and count on, whose word is good, who honors promises and never shirks responsibilities, who will be both your hero and your best friend. If you are the Principled one, you may have been badly hurt the first time around, but the next time you'll choose (or have already chosen) someone who deserves your devotion—and returns it.

PRINCIPLED SEX

Is there such a thing? Well, that's the problem. "Principled" and "sex" are two words that don't really belong in the same sentence. Principled people can be inhibited physically by their chivalry. It's often hard for them to get down and dirty, to give in to the *little* bit of selfishness and cruelty that is the spice, the yeast, in even the most loving sex.

That is at least partly compensated for by their consideration. A Principled lover wants to know what you like and is conscientious about making sure you are satisfied. She or he will patiently master the requisite technique and will become a tender and artful—if not quite an artistic—lover. Interestingly, a Principled person who has been hurt in love often becomes better in bed. That wound, that anger, opens up the darker, more irrational part of the psyche and makes him or her a less controlled, more visceral lover.

If a Principled person becomes possessed and frustrated by a cause, however, watch out. Sex can cease to exist. Every effort to soothe away stress, to unlock those iron shoulders, to offer distraction or recreation or solace will be an uphill struggle at best, and often futile. A Principled man or woman in the grip of a just grievance or crusade is as single-minded as a bulldog locked onto the throat of a burglar. He or she will hang on and worry that issue to the point of total burnout, sitting up till three in the morning, head in hands, while you lie sleepless and lonely. Often all a partner can really do is wait, while admiration sours to exasperation and finally, despair of ever getting your lover back.

But you will. The thing has to run its course. Eventually, in triumph or defeat, your hero will return to your arms . . . if they're still there. This warning to the Principled may fall on deaf ears, but don't let monomania destroy monogamy. Otherwise, when you're ready to come home from the wars, home may not be there.

②

THE PRINCIPLED AT PLAY

If the Realist at play is motivated by curiosity and adventure, and the Visionary is driven by fantasy and escape, the Principled person's mainspring is self-improvement. The free-time activities she or he is apt to enjoy most are quiet, quality time at home with family; high-culture events (this is often an NPR classical-music listener); lessons, classes, or workshops; and—though it's not exactly play—volunteering. Solving crossword puzzles or watching *Jeopardy*, with their veneer of intellectual exercise, is about as low as the Principled will sink. If this person goes on a cruise, it's probably an archeology seminar; if the family goes to the beach or the country, there will be organized bird-watching and leaf- or shell-collecting. Principled people tend to be readers, and the classics share their bookshelves with informative and exhortatory nonfiction (whether it's history or ecology, Robert Bork or Jonathan Kozol). Any morsel of free time is seized upon as an opportunity to learn or to contribute something. The same imperatives are imposed on other family members who may just want to goof off.

The Principled person values family highly and likes deliberately and thoughtfully doing things together (and that includes attending church or temple). In a sense, she or he is less selfish at play than either the absorbed, exploring Realist or the spaced-out Visionary. If the price of this together-ness is a little bit of betterment, hey—it would be churlish to complain. Principled parents' kids may squirm and whine, but when they arrive in adulthood provisioned with good work habits, good manners, and fascinating facts, they will be grateful.

PRINCIPLED SUBTYPES

■ THE LONE CRUSADER ■

noble
uncompromising
isolated
bitter

On top of a dune, hill, or cliff, there's at least room for company—and room to maneuver. A Cube that is not only above it all, but perched on its own private pedestal, suggests someone who feels unique and alone on the moral high ground—maybe even trapped up there, like a cat in a tree. We actually know two mid-level Hollywood agents whose Cubes are like this, and both perceive themselves as beleaguered islands of integrity in a sea of sleaze. (We ought to introduce them to each other.) It's a clean, noble self-image, but one that can also be isolating and embittering.

This person holds himself or herself to a uniquely high ethical standard and does not expect others to measure up. A psychoanalyst might say that the ego is identified with the ego ideal. Sticking to principle is not just a matter of pride, but a matter of identity. It's very difficult to back down from a position once taken. Lone Crusaders hate to lower themselves to bargaining and compromise, and in a negotiation, they will either prevail quickly or withdraw.

▪ THE PRINCIPLED PERFECTIONIST ▪

*all of the above
and then some*

To understand this Cube, imagine the ethical rectitude of the Lone Crusader combined with the aspiring, competitive, "soloist" and workaholic traits of the Perfectionist (see the next chapter). Few people demand this much of themselves. It's a high-stress position, conducive to both keen excellence and utter burnout.

CHAPTER 7

THE PERFECTIONIST

KEY WORDS:

ASPIRING

SOLO PERFORMER

DRIVEN

PITFALLS:

STRESS

RIVALRY

DEPRESSION

Balancing on one point, a Cube becomes something dramatically different from a regular, foursquare Cube. For one thing, it's significantly *taller* than a Cube of the same dimensions resting flat on one face. This Cube is striving skyward, sacrificing a cube's natural stability and repose to reach as high as it can. In the process, it also sheds a cube's squat sturdiness to look poised, acrobatic, gravity-defying, elegant—an improbable weightless grace achieved, like a ballerina's on point, at the cost of secret stress and tension. There's more: This Cube can no longer be stacked with other cubes. It must stand alone, in a spotlight of expectation.

It's hard (though not impossible) to lean a Ladder against it, with all those edges, jutting corners, and preoccupied slants. And all its weight is focused on one point of precision, like a solitaire diamond ready to engrave a fine line.

This is a portrait of a Perfectionist: ever striving, never arriving; a solo performer set apart by exacting standards; finicky, workaholic, private, precise. If your Cube is "on point," the goal that draws you onward may be worldly or spiritual, but it is always beyond reach, spurring ceaseless efforts that can never satisfy you. And yet this striving is the *only* thing that satisfies you—even though it also puts you at risk for depression and feelings of inadequacy, the pitfalls of this position. The Perfectionist slogan is "We are driven!" Perfectionists never feel they're doing enough, or doing it well enough. They tend to pick at the flaws and shortcomings in their own performance, even when others find it simply dazzling. And so they routinely achieve a high level of excellence while living in a perpetual state of anxiety. This makes them difficult and fascinating to be with—high-strung, temperamental, moody, charismatic, and compelling. They combine a touching fragility with a fierce will.

THE PERFECTIONIST IN THE WORLD

Notice that the Perfectionist's Cube touches the earth at only one point. This person doesn't share a lot of common ground with others; rather, she or he lives impaled on the vertical axis of excellence. The Olympic athletes' motto, "Citius, Altius, Fortius"—faster, higher, stronger—could be the Perfectionist's as well. If you are one, chances are you're so single-mindedly focused on achieving, improving, and *not failing* (not falling over, like a spun-out top) that you don't see much beyond the spotlight you always feel trained on you. While your life is a world-class performance (punctuated by impatient waits in the wings), as in a theater, the faces of the audience are in darkness. The response of others is largely irrelevant; you dismiss it because they're far too easy to please. You're basically alone up there with your most demanding coach and severest critic: yourself.

And with the intimation of perfection that ever haunts, tantalizes, and eludes you. The Realist is content with the world as it is; the Visionary is content to imagine a different one; the Principled person tries to make this one better by doggedly building from the ground up, climbing to a higher plane. But as a Perfectionist, you're not seeking an alternate or an improved reality. You want *a realized ideal.* You think from the top down; you don't see good work or physical attractiveness as better than average, but as still less than perfect. And it's not enough just to imagine perfection and invite others to imagine it (as Visionaries would if perfection, not transport, were their thing); *you've* got to make it visible, tangible, physical, actual. You've got to get it into *this* world. (Given their need to achieve flawlessness through control, no wonder Perfectionists are prone to eating disorders.) Your impossible mission is to reach up with all your will and skill, grab a piece of the perfect world of which this one is just a shoddy copy, and wrestle it down to earth, complete in every detail. The moments when you almost succeed are your moments of purest happiness.

Are Perfectionists competitive? That's an interesting question, because a familiar kind of hopeless childhood rivalry seems to be one of the ways in which Perfectionists are formed. Quite a few are younger siblings, with enough of an age gap between them and the admired and envied older sib so they feel they can never catch up. No matter how they strain upward, standing on tiptoe (like their Cube on its point), they will never be tall enough. No matter how much they learn in school, they can never match their elder's facility and mastery. Long after both are grown up, and big brother or sister has been unmasked as a mere mortal, that impossible yardstick still stands, stripped and fleshless, in the center of the Perfectionist's psyche. No actual rival is now needed to spur his or her efforts; competition has become ingrained and abstract. But if a daunting rival *does* come along, someone who appears to be—effortlessly!—everything the Perfectionist struggles to be, he or she is vulnerable to searing envy and despair.

Troubled or alcoholic families can also be fertile breeding grounds for Perfectionists. The child who has to grow up fast, who takes care of an unreliable parent, who performs impeccably in school to hide the mess at home may come to feel like a high-wire dancer without a net, or a Cube balanced precariously on one point. Control is a matter of life and death—lose your balance and it feels like you'll fall and shatter. Such children grow up to be driven, depressed high achievers, and are apt to have Perfectionist Cubes. Gloria Steinem, who has written about her childhood spent caretaking a mentally unstable mother, described her Cube this way: "It's either standing there in the distance, or it's floating—I'm not sure which—and you can see through it, even though it's on one of its points. You can just see the horizon line through the point. I'm not sure that there's any material. It may just be the outline of a cube."

❧

THE PERFECTIONIST AT WORK

Unlike the Realist, the Perfectionist is a natural-born workaholic. She or he would stay after hours even if no one else demanded it, just to get things right. Thoroughness, punctuality, precision, and detail are obsessively important. So is challenge. The Perfectionist has a "bear went over the mountain" mentality: Upon reaching the summit of one peak, she or he hardly rests before looking around for the next one to climb—preferably a higher one. Intimates may hear a lot about how overworked the Perfectionist is, or how unsure of being able to handle the latest monster task. If *you* are the Perfectionist, you may tell yourself that if you can just survive this one, that's it—you're retiring to a hammock on a tropical island. Don't believe it. A Perfectionist thrives on being stretched to the limit. "Can I do it or can't I?" becomes a cliffhanger more harrowing and thrilling than any movie, because it's real. To fail would be to fall into the abyss, so you *have* to triumph. It's a matter of life and death. Each time you succeed you feel redeemed, reborn. And then you do it all over again. Say what you like about such a life—it's not dull.

The Perfectionist style of working can be brought to any task or field. We know a university-press copy editor who opens each scholarly manuscript with the trepidation and resolve of a climber approaching

Everest. When her youngest child was in high school, she went back and finished college, which she'd interrupted to get married during World War II. Quite an achievement for a fifties homemaker? Not for this late-blooming Perfectionist, who went on to get an M.A. and then a Ph.D. in English—in *her* fifties. She is a second daughter. *Her* second daughter is the only one of six siblings whose Cube is "on point," as well as the family's only degreed professional. After finishing a premed course, medical school, her internship and residency, this Perfectionist went on to complete an advanced fellowship in infectious diseases while raising three kids. The itch never stays scratched; the restless need for achievement remains unslaked by each success.

Many Perfectionists prefer to work within a tradition where they can measure themselves against an established scale of excellence. Classical music and ballet, Shakespearean theater, Olympic athletics, and conservative professions like science and medicine all have well-defined ideals and rigorous criteria for entry and advancement. There is almost no ambiguity about what perfection is, how far you are from it, and what is the next step. If at first you don't make that jump, find that vein, or play the "Moonlight Sonata" without any wrong notes, you can just practice, practice, practice and then try, try again. Only with the security of advanced skill are you given a little latitude for your individuality, and even then it's a small variation on a grand old theme.

All this structure is comforting to Perfectionists; it makes them feel less alone—part of a fellowship across time—and relieves their anxious need to know how they're doing and what they *should* be doing. Originality in a

Perfectionist is a special torment, because the master image and the measure of progress exist nowhere but in his or her own mind. For the painter Cézanne, the sculptor Giacometti, and several of the Abstract Expressionists, the vocation of art meant a lifetime of trying and failing, trying and failing to reproduce in paint or metal what they could see with their mind's eye. What looks to us like a great body of work is, to the Perfectionist artist, a record of greater and lesser failures, the waste products of longing.

In a company or institution, the Perfectionist does not work very comfortably either above or under others—or beside them, for that matter. If you have this stand-alone, unstackable Cube, you need to control your own domain of work so that the quality of the product directly reflects your own standards and efforts. A supervisor who rushes or micromanages you, subordinates who do sloppy work, teammates who crowd you and average your contribution into the group effort—all will cut down on your job satisfaction and productivity. On the other hand, you can work your whole life long for a supervisor who trusts you to run your own shop and appreciates the quality of the results. We suspect that many a treasured executive secretary is a Perfectionist who lucked into just such a spot.

As a supervisor yourself, you don't like to delegate and you do tend to micromanage, because you don't trust most employees to do things as well as you want them done. (Anyone who's worked for a Perfectionist boss knows how annoying this can be, because this boss has a narrow definition of "doing things well": "doing them the way I would do them.") Only if you discover that you have a fellow Perfectionist working for you can you sometimes relax and let go of the reins. As a leader, you are an inspiring (and sometimes intimidating) example more than a hands-on manager and troubleshooter. Let's face it: You work best either alone in your own space, or out in front. Perfectionists are solo performers of two kinds: those who suffer from stage fright and need to perform in private, and those who flourish up in front of others as teachers, speakers, or divas.

❧

THE PERFECTIONIST IN LOVE

At work, the Perfectionist converts insecurity into performance, enthralled by the tidy drama of proving himself or herself over and over again. But you can't "do" love that way. Emotions—one's own and the other person's—can't be controlled by will or skill. In matters of the heart, the Perfectionist formula for mastering anxiety is useless. And this makes their private lives tumultuous.

Driven to try to control the uncontrollable, a Perfectionist instinctively works with the materials at hand, honing helpless moods into "smart" emotional weapons. All's fair in the primal struggle to snare attention and extract reassurance: slam doors, make scenes, shed tears, withdraw into sultry silences that are impossible to ignore. As if that weren't enough, all this heavy weather is punctuated by virtual absences—a Perfectionist on a deadline might as well not be there—and by the periodic depressions that are the Perfectionist's way of resting (this person only feels justified in doing nothing when he or she absolutely *can't* do anything). If you are the Perfectionist, you know that nothing your lover says or does can ever soothe you for long. If you are the lover, you are by turns fascinated, irritated, mystified, and exhausted. Among the most attractive people on the planet, Perfectionists will hook you bad and then put you through the wringer. Some partners learn to retaliate by withholding attention or approval, sure-fire ways to throw a Perfectionist off center.

The truth is that behind their formidably accomplished facade, Perfectionists are needy, and afraid of abandonment. That's one of the things they flee by keeping so busy, because they can easily lose their balance in love. Powerful hungers, fears, and jealousies are unleashed as soon as a lover is allowed to become important. A securely married Perfectionist may obsess and speculate for *years* about a spouse's long-gone high school or college sweetheart. The Perfectionist in love craves exclusivity and sensitive attentiveness (the lover should, ideally, be a mind reader). This is a private person who would much rather be alone together, the center of a lover's attention, than go to a party or have friends over for dinner. The gregarious Realist, who likes to hang out and party, frequently frustrates this Perfectionist need for the reassurance of undivided attention. A Visionary partner's fantasies may be perceived as spectral rivals, or as an implied critique of the Perfectionist's inadequacies; the Visionary's susceptibility to infatuation poses a constant, simmering threat. A Principled lover can be driven batty when the Perfectionist's gnawing insecurity resists the most earnest reassurances.

Deep down, it's the same life-and-death drama the Perfectionist acts out at work, only instead of "Can I do this or can't I?" it's "Do you love me or don't you?" And deeper still, "Am I worthy? Do I deserve love?" The dizzying height of Perfectionists' aspirations measures the depth of their self-doubt. To believe they are any good, they've got to be the best; to believe they're "the one," they have to be "the only."

Of course, these needs are, by definition, insatiable. And eventually Perfectionists figure that out. With time, and sometimes therapy, they mellow a bit; they develop a sense of humor about themselves, or at least a wry perspective on their own drivenness. They don't exactly relax, but they lose that sense of "do or die." Unlike Visionaries, whose dreams never quit, mature Perfectionists eventually give up on romantic love as a primary source of the affirmation they need. It's just too hard on themselves and their lovers, and they realize that it's not realistic. Work—and the driven Perfectionist brand of play—are more appropriate arenas for this ritual struggle, because here the Perfectionist has some control over the outcome. (And young children's love can be a balm to the Perfectionist soul, because it really *is* unconditional and exclusive—there's only one Mom or Dad.) With this realization, Perfectionists can become quite self-contained and self-sufficient. They can live alone or companionably side by side with a partner, often going their separate ways. Now and then they may still say, "I want your undivided attention," but at least as often it will be, "I want to be alone."

PERFECTIONIST SEX

There's a don't-touch-me quality about this Cube. Physically fastidious, standoffish, and something of a control freak, the Perfectionist is rarely very comfortable with the flesh, especially if it isn't perfect (and whose flesh is?). We noted the high incidence of eating disorders among Perfectionists, at least the ones *we* know; it would be interesting to see if they're also extra susceptible to the promises of plastic surgery. Silicone breast implants deaden the erotic sensitivity of the nipple, so women who get them care more about how they look than what they feel. It would be just like a Perfectionist to sacrifice subjective pleasure for objective perfection.

Not all Perfectionists do that, though. After all, passionate sex can be a potent source of reassurance. At least it's one time when you're alone together and your lover is focused totally on you (or so you hope!). Orgasm then can be, like achievement, a brief, shining moment of arrival, affirmation, and release from anxiety. Its emotional meaning is more important than its sensuality.

A Perfectionist in a passionate relationship tends to be private and possessive about it. She or he may not want to show affection in public, and—if only to downplay bodily flaws—may prefer making love under covers or in the dark. Rituals of gradual approach and getting-in-the-mood are very important, since the Perfectionist needs time to shift down and patient wooing-away from the stresses of the day. If you just touch a tightly wound Perfectionist, she or he will jump and shudder like a skittish horse. There are days and moods when unwinding is out of the question, and the Perfectionist is literally untouchable. Even at their most loving, even as devoted, affectionate parents, Perfectionists tend not to be cuddly, touchy-feely people. A quick, shy, upper-body hug and an air kiss is their idea of getting physical with family and friends.

THE PERFECTIONIST AT PLAY

When Perfectionists take the time to play at all, they like to play the same way they work: pick a challenging, competitive skill and work at perfecting it. It might be golf, or chess, or mountaineering, or martial arts, or equestrian show jumping—something that requires coordination, concentration, and practice and in which there is always room for improvement. Or it might be redecorating rooms or building cabinets—doing something to make your home that much closer to perfect. The Perfectionist at play is a serious amateur, not a happy dabbler like the Realist, who is content to get pretty good at half a dozen things. The Perfectionist will take on more than one pastime only if she or he can find the time to master each of them. We've all heard of wealthy people who make it their project to become serially or simultaneously brilliant at polo, painting, flying, French haute cuisine, skiing, and string quartets, but for most Perfectionists, any one of the above would be enough.

If you live with one, you know how hard it is to get a Perfectionist to veg out for more than a few minutes. This is not a beach sitter; no one could be further from a couch potato. If you're the Perfectionist, you know how hard it is to explain to others that your flesh crawls when you're forced to be idle. You'd rather do the books or mop the floors. Doing is your way of being. When you're not busy proving or improving something, you feel yourself disappearing.

How can a non-Perfectionist get a Perfectionist to take a vacation, or even take in a movie? First, catch him or her coming right off the completion of a project—or at least at the end of a good day's work. As every Perfectionist will ruefully acknowledge, this is the one moment when they feel briefly entitled to relax and celebrate. Second, if you can share your Perfectionist's interest in, say, golf or skiing, you don't have to be as serious about it as she or he is. You can putz around on the bunny slopes while the Perfectionist practices stem christies. (But God help you if your Perfectionist is a sailor, because then you'll have to crew, and you'll get yelled at for coiling ropes—er, sheets—sloppily.) And third, you can strike a deal with Perfectionists. If they'll come out and play in the afternoon (and they really need that replenishment), you promise them the whole morning to work—*undisturbed*. A word that's music to Perfectionists' ears, for the point of this Cube is focus and concentration.

The Perfectionist

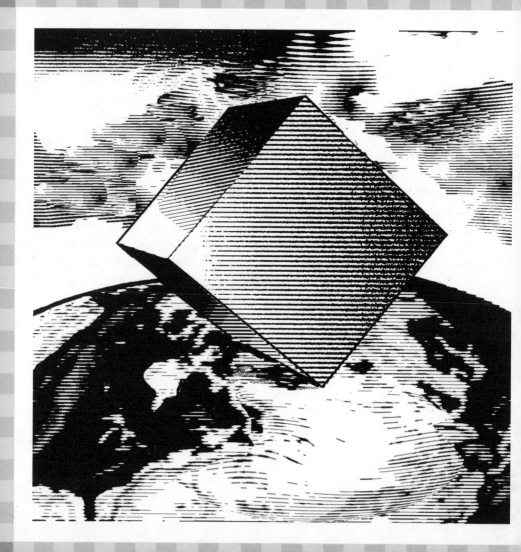

CHAPTER 8

THE
EXPATRIATE

KEY WORDS:

BETWEEN

RESOURCEFUL

ADAPTABLE

PITFALLS:

SPLIT

ROOTLESS

OVERLOOKED

The Cube standing on its edge is our most dramatic case of an unexpected yet unequivocal message from the collective unconscious, a fascinating glimpse into the logic of the deep mind. We might have guessed, based on the "pun principle," that this Cube would represent someone "edgy," or "on edge," or even "cutting-edge." Not so. Without exception, *everyone* who has described this Cube to us so far has been . . . an immigrant!

Or an emigrant, depending on which side of the borderline you're looking from. Someone whose life is balanced between two lands, two worlds; who can fully live in neither; whose identity is founded not on some patch of solid ground but precisely on the borderline. This person's psyche is dominated and defined by the dividing line between then and now, here and there, mother tongue and new language. Out of an infinite variety of raw material, the experience of immigration evidently smelts a distinctive personality type: dual, adaptable, resourceful, precarious, rootless. It is a type that can only become more common as our globe grows ever smaller and its denizens more mobile. All it takes is an overseas assignment or a cross-cultural romance.

Not all immigrants, however, have Cubes "on edge." People who have a strong sense of vocation carry their home ground with them wherever they go. For instance, we know an accomplished sculptor and jeweler from Romania whose Realist Cube survived his move to the United States. He lives in his craft now, as he did before. (His mother-in-law, however, who came to New York to help care for her grandson, has a classic edge-balancing Cube.) People who immigrated two or three decades ago, who've married and put down real roots in their new homeland, do not generally have Cubes on edge; nor do adults who made the move in childhood. This is the Cube of someone who was transplanted as a teenager or adult, and relatively recently; who is no longer at home in the "old country," but not yet at home in the new. Frequently, it's someone who still travels back and forth (the sculptor's mother-in-law spends summers in Romania), and having friends and family in both countries intensifies his or her divided allegiance and dual consciousness.

It's conceivable that this could also be the Cube of someone who's "in between" in some other way—biracial, bicultural, bicoastal, bi- or transsexual, the child of intermarriage, a career-changer, or a worker in an interdisciplinary field. If so, however, we have yet to see it. Let us know if you do. Meanwhile, as the Cube of the Expatriate, this position demonstrates that our place on earth can shape our personality just as decisively as personality shapes our place in the world.

◉

THE EXPATRIATE IN THE WORLD

With poetic economy, the line where the Cube's edge meets the sand compresses into one image the division down the center of the Expat psyche; the sharp axe blow of severance from native ground; and the tenuous, teetery feeling of living on strange new ground. Heavy with the memories and mores of the old life, uncertain of step in the new, the Expatriate must perform a balancing act, carrying an alien identity lightly through uncomprehending surroundings. When you're an immigrant, not only is your angle on life different from everyone's around you, but your personal past and cultural heritage are largely invisible to them. What they see is the sketchy new identity: the good sport with an eager smile and a clumsy accent—a stereotype. Your ability to travel light with a lonely load (shared only by others in your particular Expat community) is only one of many paradoxes and dualities of this position. Your point of contact with the earth is a threshold; you are always simultaneously departing and arriving.

More than any other Cube, this one is Janus-faced. Everything about this position has two sides. Living in two cultures and two languages is both a strength and a weakness, both a split and a synthesis. Polish-American writer Eva Hoffman titled her memoir of immigration *Lost in Translation,* but much is found in translation as well. Misunderstandings may abound, yet intelligence is exercised and strengthened. Your repertoire of concepts and perspectives is not just doubled but multiplied, as your struggle to focus the eyes of two cultures is rewarded with 3-D vision. Not only can you see life as both your old and your new countrymen do, but juxtaposing the two gives you a new depth of insight that's both dispassionate and compassionate, that sees through local oddities to human universals. This combination of versatility and penetration is a precious, often untapped resource that will become much more valued, indeed sought after, in the twenty-first century.

Immigrating is a kind of death and rebirth in life. Even people in their sixties often rise like phoenixes to the challenge with youthful adaptability and renewed mental agility. Expatriates' emotions are every bit as dual and ambivalent as their minds. A zest for adventure cohabits with nostalgia, optimism with melancholy, enterprise with the pangs of exile. This bittersweet condition *becomes* their identity, until many of them would no longer choose to live anywhere *but* on the edge, among the new nomadic tribe whose natural habitat is the airport, and who may foreshadow the future of humanity.

THE EXPATRIATE AT WORK

There are several varieties of Expatriate experience in the workplace, depending on how voluntarily a person left home in the first place, and how transferable his or her old skills are to the new place. Those who took wing reluctantly—only because life at home had become unbearable due to war, disaster, destitution, or oppression—tend to suffer the most dislocation in their working lives. Old class and educational distinctions are leveled as farmers and laborers work side by side with former engineers and doctors in whatever menial jobs are available. Language problems limit the kind of work most new immigrants can do, and much advanced training—such as in law, medicine, or education—doesn't "translate" easily. So it's not at all uncommon to find professors swabbing bathrooms and mathematicians being nannies.

As a result, the reluctant immigrant's whole vocational identity may be left behind, and coworkers may have no idea of this taciturn person's true knowledge, skill, and sophistication. The split between languages and cultures runs right down the center of his or her daily life, sharply dividing the rudimentary relationships at work from the rich and complex life with friends at home. You don't have to be an immigrant to experience this split. Anyone bicultural—ethnic and minority Americans, or even women—can feel underrated or stereotyped at work, and that their human skills are overlooked and underused in the strictly task-oriented workplace.

By contrast, economic immigrants, who made their move in pursuit of opportunity, usually thrive at work. Their skills and interests tend to be of the robustly universal kind that can flourish anywhere: food, construction, mechanics, electronics, trade, and business. And the same drive that propelled them out of a dead-end life makes them hard and eager workers who will do whatever it takes—wash lettuce at five A.M., work twelve-hour days and attend night school—to be a success.

As native elites move into the information economy and less-skilled natives into service jobs, more and more of the world's cabdrivers, grocers, newsstand proprietors, restaurateurs, export-importers, wholesalers, travel agents, electronics-repair and construction workers are highly motivated immigrant small-business entrepreneurs living in their own island communities. Theirs is the vitality that virtually built the United States and is now revitalizing the "old countries" of the world, whether through immigration from country to country or from village to city. Living in neighborhoods that are satellites of Port-au-Prince or Bombay, limiting contact with the surrounding culture and use of the second language to what's strictly necessary for work, these immigrants minimize the conflicts of their status and may well have Realist Cubes. (It's their children who may feel divided.)

And finally, there's the new nomadic elite of businesspeople who go to work halfway around the world, either because their company sends them, or because they're attracted by the heady blend of opportunity and adventure. These Expatriates deliberately seek the duality and rootlessness that is forced on involuntary exiles. Their success in the transnational economy sheds a new, appreciative light on the mental "hybrid vigor" that has made immigrants not just refugees from the breakdown of nations, but the pioneers of a new global mind-set and lifestyle. The border is the new frontier; the interface between cultures is now the "hot spot" of human evolution. And the Expatriate has that interface right inside his or her head! So if you are one, or if you have one working for you, you may be overlooking a remarkable resource right under your nose.

An Expatriate has special strengths to bring to any working situation: adaptability, determination, and most important of all, *multiple* perspectives. He or she not only brings the concepts of a different culture to the problem-solving mix, but through having to negotiate between two realities has become a skilled intermediary—acutely aware of differing points of view and often adept at bridging, reconciling, or synthesizing them. Depending on other abilities and interests, this person will excel at work that does not try to deny but actively depends on "betweenness": as a translator or interpreter; a negotiator or conflict mediator; in travel, import/export, or international sales; as a teacher, counselor, intermediary, or marketer to newer immigrants; as a liaison between communities or departments.

For a valuable contribution in any job, ask the Expatriate how it would be done differently where she or he comes from. (For example, businesses are discovering that the much more social style of doing business in non-Western countries—the importance of hospitality, the ritual of tea and conversation before getting down to brass tacks—is well worth the time it appears to "waste.") Solicit his or her observations of your workplace—the Expat sees from a different angle and may point out something crucial that you've missed. And whenever possible, give him or her the responsibility for orienting newcomers. This person has found out the hard way what others need to know, and can speed and smooth a new member's integration into the team.

☙

THE EXPATRIATE IN LOVE

Nothing disrupts a person's life as much as moving from one country to another. How, then, could it fail to disrupt your love life? The borderline bisecting the Expatriate psyche often becomes a barrier or chasm between lovers, whether the separation is physical or cultural. As an Expat you may be attached to someone who's still "back home"; you may migrate *with* a mate whose adjustment to the move is way out of sync with yours; or you may fall in love with someone from the new culture who doesn't know the half of who you are. Existing relationships, while they offer comfort amid strangeness, have to reinvent themselves under stress; new relationships, while they offer the attraction of the exotic, also feature its flip side—mutual incomprehension. The "borderline," by putting hurdles in love's path, can either trip it up or make it stronger. But at the same time, love is the great dismantler of boundaries: Where do we learn a new language fastest but in bed? If work brings different kinds of people within range of each other, it's love that closes the distance and leaps the gap, twining two strands of cultural DNA together to engender the life-forms of the future.

Remember, love—at least in its early, passionate stages—actually thrives on obstacles. Expatriates' love lives tend to be intense and dramatic, cleft by tragic separations, strung taut with longing, electrified by attraction to the strange. As usual, the Expat condition brackets both extremes: Arriving in a strange land, you can feel acutely lonely; later, you may find yourself a special object of romantic pursuit. But it's a mixed blessing, because it's not for *you* so much as for your sheer Otherness, your adorable accent and the sexual reputation (deserved or not) of your nationality. You can capitalize on that for a while, but it's vaguely insulting—and still lonely. Eventually, though, if you're with the same person long enough, the glamour of difference wears off. You're each left facing not some sort of alien angel, but another human being with whom you have a few more grounds for misunderstanding than usual. This disillusionment spells either the end of the relationship or the beginning of the real action.

Loving someone from another culture is one of the most mind-bending, mind-expanding experiences there is. It's hard enough to thrash out issues like food, religion, politics, and child-rearing when you come from different families, never mind different *countries*. At the same time (and here's that other side), the friction of cultural differences makes each of you more conscious and individual. To meet your lover, you have to come out of your culture and play in the open.

It's risky, like all improvisation: The terrain is unmapped, the script unwritten. You have to question all your assumptions and distinguish what you really choose to believe from what has merely been drilled into you. Paradoxically, in gaining this perspective on your own culture, you also come to appreciate it more. It's what *you* bring to the table. Meanwhile, your lover's heritage gets under your skin, into your taste buds and your musical ear. Your repertoire of jokes, dishes, holidays, and handy idioms (not to mention swear words) doubles. You both get the goodies not only of two cultures, but of the third, motley one you are creating together. The dividing line becomes the cutting edge.

In short, to love an Expatriate is to become one.

EXPATRIATE SEX

And to love across borders is to discover that sex isn't just sex, a discovery that naturally generates both passion and confusion. While there's less room for variation than in cuisines, sexuality, too, is shaped and flavored by custom. So when approaching a lover of an unfamiliar culture, you never know quite what you're getting. A sexual practice that's standard operating procedure for you may be novel or shocking to your lover, or vice versa. For example, sexually sophisticated women in some parts of Eastern Europe would be insulted if you so much as suggested oral sex. And there are even people in this world (some African tribes, for instance) who find *kissing* disgusting.

But the most interesting differences are the subtle ones, the shadings added by each culture's pervasive attitudes toward men and women, control and abandon, flesh and feeling. How do potential lovers approach each other? (Some of the world's most macho men are its greatest artists of seduction—masters of the look, the wink, the tender caress with the same hand that'll give you a whack when the honeymoon's over.) Can they loll in bed for hours, or are they anxious to get it over with? Is sensual touching an art for art's sake, or just a means to an end? What happens afterward?

THE EXPATRIATE AT PLAY

One of the best things about being, or being with, an Expat—at least from an American's point of view—is that cultures other than ours have preserved the fine art of doing nothing. Or at least what looks to *us* like "nothing." When we USsies get together with friends or go on vacation, we almost always have to Do Something in a big way: go to a movie, rent a movie, go bowling, go snowboarding, read something, make something, learn something, solve a puzzle, knit a sweater, yadda yadda yadda . . . Americans even "do" drugs! Of course, we're not the only people on earth who enjoy activities—but we *are* the only ones who seem unable to stop. The compulsiveness of our drive to Do has a Calvinist, capitalist quality: We feel we have to be productive even at leisure. Activity this driven may be fun, but it's also a flight from ourselves and each other.

In almost any other culture on earth, people spend a lot of their free time *just being* together. They sit in cafés or in each other's kitchens, slowly sip their coffee or tea or wine or beer, joke, laugh, and make conversation. In our culture, only old hippies, drunks, hopeless Visionaries, and the un- and underemployed do this. It's called "hanging out" or being a "slacker," and it is regarded as a reprehensible form of laziness. And yet, at such seemingly pointless parties and gatherings, quite a lot is actually going on: Civilization is being made, like a patchwork quilt. These are schmoozing bees, grassroots salons in which the fine fabric of the common mind is worked on, joke by joke, thought by thought, stitch by stitch.

If you are lucky enough to be or to know an Expatriate, you've already been infected with this wondrous virus of creative idleness, and you have added hanging out to your repertoire of ways of having fun. It is now your responsibility to propagate this virus, to help it burrow to the very heart of American society, so that this most subtle and vital of pastimes—the very lifeblood of our humanity—isn't wiped out, but is carried along as our culture of fast-food joints and theme parks tramples the earth.

CHAPTER 9

THE
UNSUNG HERO

KEY WORDS:

MYSTERY

HIDDEN POWER

INFLUENCE

SELF-SUFFICIENCY

PITFALLS:

OBSCURITY

EXPLOITATION BY OTHERS

LONELINESS

very now and then, when you instruct someone to describe the cube, she or he will tell you, "It's a pyramid." When this first happened to us, we wondered if the association of pyramids with deserts was so strong it was overriding the instructions. Hearing "desert," maybe some people were just jumping to the clichéd conclusion.

But our growing experience had taught us that nothing in this game is accidental. So we began looking to see if our "pyramidal" friends had any traits in common. Indeed, they did—and clichéd thinking wasn't one of them. On the contrary, these people had cultivated deep, complex, far-reaching minds—though you'd hardly know it from their gracious, self-deprecating manner. Very private in personal life, and preferring to operate outside the limelight at work, they weren't exactly secretive, but they did seem content for their true stature to remain the best-kept secret. Making major contributions while taking minimal credit, they were "out of sight" in both senses of the term.

But why a pyramid? Certainly pyramids, too, are mysterious and remote. Their sunny, cryptic surface conceals so much: the secret of their origin, the true extent of their powers, and the hidden cubic chamber at their heart that enshrines the royal personage. But this image didn't *really* click for us till we realized that a pyramid could be one visible corner of a much larger Cube buried underground. With the Unsung Hero, what you see isn't what you get—it's just the tip of the iceberg.

❧

THE UNSUNG HERO IN THE WORLD

If you are anything like the Unsung Heroes we know, you've done quite a bit of solitary thinking—possibly of a spiritual or philosophical nature. You've worked out a complex, comprehensive, and original worldview, but you keep it to yourself and for yourself. It serves as the hidden source for your unusual insights, which can make people do a double take, coming as they do from someone so sportsmanlike and self-effacing. If there ever was the diametrical opposite of a diva, it's you. (Which is especially fascinating since, if your Cube were raised aboveground, it would be in the position of that classic diva, the Perfectionist.) You have a quiet confidence and substance, but you prefer to deflect attention toward others, and to let even your ideas and contributions shine on their own without your name and face splashed across them.

With their own feelings held in reserve, Unsung Heroes can achieve a dispassion and neutrality that makes them natural diplomats and peacemakers. The word that keeps coming to mind is "civilized." Just try and tempt one to gossip or backbite—you'll be frustrated. They'll almost never say a bad word about someone else, even someone you think has used or wronged them. They are wonderful at listening and drawing others out in a flattering way. It isn't false flattery, it's the art of shining warm interest on the best of someone. You will never have a more intelligent and sympathetic audience than an Unsung Hero—and you'll never know for sure what he or she *really* thinks of you. Good manners make good cover for a keen observer, but the Pyramid keeps its own counsel. As information-storage systems go, stone is opaque.

Unsung Heroes are reluctant to talk about themselves, and they never, ever complain. If you are one, you probably don't easily discuss childhood, family, or feelings unless it's with your closest friends—and even then, you may distance it with style and humor, or deftly turn it around so *they* end up talking about themselves. "Let it all hang out" is the one thing you'd rather die than do. Playing the Cube may embarrass you, and you'll no doubt keep its meaning to yourself. ("Hmmm, that's interesting," is the most a freshly cubed Unsung Hero has ever said to us.) In an age of public confession, therapeutic sincerity, and full disclosure to the point of overexposure, this antique sense of privacy can act as a cloak of invisibility. For better and for worse, you can accomplish wonders without ever attracting much attention. The Unsung Hero is like a dark star—a heavenly body astronomers can't see, but know is there by the effects of its gravitation. You have that kind of mass and influence. Only you can answer the question: Is it enough?

©

THE UNSUNG HERO AT WORK

Unsung Heroes are the people who lay the groundwork and donate many of the ideas for which others get the glory. They are editors and ghostwriters; aides, assistants, and advisors; confidants and nurturers; campaign managers, speechwriters, and strategists—the "power behind the throne." If that role has a feminine connotation, consider that traditionally, being an Unsung Hero was one of the few ways an intelligent woman could—indirectly—make her mark on the world. Such women are the dark stars of history, the wives, mothers, and uncredited collaborators of legions of Great Men. Their patron saint is Aspasia, the lover and advisor without whose counsel Pericles of Athens would not have been as great an orator.

But you don't have to be a woman to aid and comfort genius. Leonard Woolf, George Henry Lewes, George Eliot's companion, and many a diva's lover-manager belong in this company, too. If indeed "it takes one to know one," that shadowy figure in the background of great achievement must possess his or her own kind of genius. But it is a genius for "partnering," in the ballet sense, or being an accompanist, as in jazz—providing the perfect, unobtrusive setting in which another can shine. The Unsung Hero's motto might well be "Always the bridesmaid, never the bride."

Before you rush indignantly to their defense, though, remember: This is often a role the Unsung Hero has *chosen*. It's significant that pyramids are almost always seen from a distance. When we ask, "How big is the cube? How near or far away?" (see page 178), we're asking about your perspective on yourself. Unsung Heroes see themselves matter-of-factly as large and powerful, but *in the background*, part of a much bigger picture—and a long vista of time. They are very, very hard workers who like to lose themselves in the process of work, then stand back and take an anonymous pride in the product, like medieval craftsmen contemplating a cathedral: "Only I will know I carved that gargoyle." They prefer to skip the stage so many people live for—the Oscar ceremony, as it were. To them, the fuss over personalities is distasteful and misplaced.

But don't get us wrong. That's not to say Unsung Heroes are uninterested in power. On the contrary: They are found near it, in its shadow, far more often than could be accounted for by chance. (Pyramids, of course, are associated with kings.) In fact, they are power's "yin" side, without which it would be all brass and bluster. They cool down its excesses, carry out its directives, mediate between the temperamental Star and the world. Every president, four-star general, dictator, and diva needs one. We're thinking of a retired career diplomat we know who now does conflict-resolution work for a former president, and the features editor of a magazine who ran interference between writers and her capricious editor in chief while quietly writing much of the magazine herself. The Unsung Hero *belongs* close to power, refining and guiding its actions, keeping it linked (as pyramids do kings) to the real spiritual sources of worldly might.

To be content in your job if your Cube is a pyramid, what you require from your boss is respect and trust, far more than attention or praise. You find close supervision intrusive and insulting; you like to be given a task or mission and then left alone to do it as you see fit. And you expect the same self-reliance from those under *your* supervision. Nothing annoys you more than subordinates who can't think for themselves and need constant, detailed instructions.

As for your boss . . . you'd never admit it in a million years, but you're smarter than he or she is, and you know it. (Okay, okay, so maybe "smarter" isn't quite the right word—deeper, more reflective. A front man or woman needs to be raw, bold, impulsive, shrewd, self-promoting, and gut-guided. You provide the "on second thought.") You work way above and beyond the call of duty, figuring out better ways to do what you were told, fleshing out your skeleton orders with your own originality and creativity. Your boss will come to rely on this and will get used to taking credit for it. You don't mind that—what matters to you is that your ideas have an influence, not whose name is on them. But be careful—*don't* get short-changed when it comes to money! Unsung Heroes provide their extraordinary services so self-effacingly that they are often taken for granted and shamelessly exploited. We hate to say this, but it's their own fault. To be valued at even half of what you're worth—and just to be able to pay your bills—you may have to do what you hate most: call attention to yourself. A little strike will do the trick nicely. After a week of trying to function without you, your boss will be in shock.

There may come a time in an Unsung Hero's life when he or she decides to step forward and be recognized—an undertaking as major as unearthing a pyramid-sized Cube. For instance, that magazine editor recently gave notice at her job—three months' notice, typically, to gently wean her boss—and has resolved to return to an unfinished novel. No one is more deserving of having their praises sung. If you're a Hero going public, however, be prepared to encounter strong inner resistance. Attention to the self is, for you, almost taboo. You're never going to write the great confessional memoir. On the other hand, you're the kind of person fiction is made for. If you *still* feel naked, try a pseudonym.

☻

THE UNSUNG HERO IN LOVE

There's something about an Unsung Hero that is always alone, even when he or she is in a long and fond relationship. This person learned early in life to be as self-reliant and self-sufficient as a well-provisioned ship, often in reaction to parents who were either indifferent or intrusive (both are ways of ignoring a child's real needs). As in the drawing of the mostly buried cube, the greater part of the Unsung Hero—his or her whole emotional life—has "gone underground." The corner that pokes up is intellect and reason, bless its little pointed head. This makes intimacy difficult, for it requires self-disclosure and a sharing of the emotions Unsung Heroes have learned to keep to themselves.

The result may be one of two life patterns. After a relationship or two fails, the Unsung Hero may withdraw into living alone, growing ever more set in the serene, stoic ways of solitude and ever rustier at the hinges for opening up. Why go through the pain of reviving mummified longings? If love does come along, it may seem to demand too much—unless it's the love of someone just as independent who is willing to coexist, not mingle. Loneliness is held at bay, and this life made possible, by wonderful friendships, for this is a gifted, gallant friend who inspires and returns fierce devotion. What's friendship, after all, but love at the perfect distance—by your side, but not prying into your heart?

And that's precisely the kind of love that does work for many Unsung Heroes. They marry, have children, surround themselves with family—and still, somehow, they're alone. They are fair, gentle, rational, witty, faithful, and affectionate—*civilized*—yet their mate and kids rarely know what they're thinking or feeling because they don't say it or show it. Unsung Heroes become deeply absorbed in their work, which may also require physical absences. "Commuter marriage" can be perfectly comfortable for them; they don't feel solitude as a deprivation. It's their spouse who may feel deprived and lonely even when the Hero is at home.

We know an Unsung Hero, male, who's devotedly married to a Visionary. In the early years of their marriage, they physically lived together, but he was "gone" in his important work much of the time. Starved for romantic intimacy, she finally had a reckless affair. Their marriage survived, and he learned to be more attentive to her needs (if not more expressive of his own)—but now he's doing important work in a *different city*. And she? She's become a successful romance novelist, and after their weekends together she's content to see him go so she can snuggle back into her fantasy world—Visionary heaven. Happy ending.

The moral of the story: If you love an Unsung Hero, find a hobby! No, really: It does help to have some emotional self-sufficiency of your own. This person isn't cold, cruel, or at all inclined to infidelity. She or he is simply a profound introvert wrapped in a very convincing extrovert. If you don't pry, one day you may be entrusted with a peek into the royal chamber. There you will see a poignant and eerie sight: the heart of someone who has accepted that we are all ultimately alone.

SEX AND THE UNSUNG HERO

This stoic, self-sufficient person often has his or her passions so well under control that they're almost banished from conscious life. Sexuality has become a banked fire driving the locomotive of work. A passion for good food, which offers physical pleasure without the emotional danger, may be the visible tip of a sizable, buried sensuality and need. For some strange reason, the Unsung Heroes we know have in common a certain immobility and alienation from their bodies. They are, or aspire to be, the sort of evolved, cerebral beings you see on *Star Trek,* talking about the regrettable necessity of inhabiting these material vehicles. They've moved upstairs into their heads, where the sense of taste (in both senses of the word) is their solace for Spartan rations below the neck.

Call it the Mr. Spock syndrome. Spock had legions of fans who were just *sure* that a passionate Earthling simmered under his beautiful deadpan Vulcan mien. Each fan imagined being the only one both irresistible and trustworthy enough to tap into that molten core. Like Mr. Spock, Unsung Heroes both fascinate and frustrate. They can be so cool it burns. There's the sense that a secret panel must be hidden somewhere, which—if you could only find and press it—would turn your Pyramid into a volcano (to switch metaphors from *Star Trek* to Indiana Jones). On second thought, is that such a good idea? Fortunately or not, that panel is *almost* impossible to find. For lovers turned on by challenges, this one has the difficulty level of a Chinese puzzle or a 3.2 Olympic dive.

@

THE UNSUNG HERO AT PLAY

The Unsung (in contrast to the Undead, who at least need blood) are as self-contained at play as in all else—that is, when they have time for play at all. They're usually too contented and busy working. No type needs leisure less. It's another peculiar link to the Perfectionist: They're both workaholics, but that's where the resemblance ends. For Perfectionists, success is always in doubt, and everything's personal; their workaholism is anxiety-driven and results in periodic exhaustion. For Unsung Heroes, almost nothing is personal, and they have a modest but solid confidence in their capabilities. They're driven (believe it or not) by a wish to be of service, and *maybe* by a flight from the mess of the personal. But there's nothing joyless about it. They're in their element at work and draw nearly endless energy from it. Only the rare physical illness can stop them, and it's often the only sign that they need replenishment.

That said, when they do have time off (between assignments? in airports?) they are perfectly able to entertain themselves. They are voracious readers. They knit. They cook gourmet meals for their friends. They *think*. And, typically, they travel to distant places, often in pursuit of a spiritual quest or a fascination with history. As befits their Cube, Unsung Heroes are drawn to ancient and remote civilizations, times and places where power was based on something more subtle, cosmic, and elegant than money and celebrity. They feel like old souls homesick for more cultivated surroundings. In an instinctive attempt to recapture that, they may spend hours of their leisure time learning languages, or arts like calligraphy or the Japanese tea ceremony.

CHAPTER 10

THE
RECEPTIVE

KEY WORDS:

INTROSPECTIVE

NURTURING

PSYCHIC

PITFALLS:

OVERANALYSIS

GARRULITY

LONELINESS

n Japan, we're told, *space* is regarded as a positive entity, not just an absence of things. It's one reason for the spare, exquisite proportions of Japan's traditional interior design and gardens. Where Westerners tend to stuff a room with furniture, the Japanese may be said to sculpt space.

And so may the person who sees his or her Cube not as a solid object, but as a cubic hole in the ground, often filled with water. (Related Cubes—if not quite Receptive subtypes—are aboveground Cubes magically made out of space or water, and any Cube with the emphasis on its interior. Whatever the position of your Cube, if *inside* it is where the action is, you may have some Receptive traits as well.)

As negative space—a cube-shaped shaft or chamber cut into the earth—this position is rarer than Rh-negative blood, at least in the West. (We'll be fascinated to see if it crops up more often in a space-conscious culture like Japan's.) Right away, it suggests someone whose way of thinking and sense of self are contrary to convention, the photographic negative of what you'd expect. As an extroverted culture, what we expect is a solid ego that juts up, displacing space. The Receptive person proposes instead: What if I *am* space, waiting to be filled? It's a move as provocative as architect Maya Lin's when, in place of a high, heroic statue, she designed a Vietnam Veterans Memorial that descends into the earth. Instead of being told the war's official meaning, you are invited down and in to discover a meaning for yourself. The Receptive Cube portrays someone whose identity *is* his or her interiority: the inner experience, not the outward appearance; subjectivity, not image.

@

THE RECEPTIVE IN THE WORLD

In one sense, the Receptive person is like an Unsung Hero, only even more so: This Cube is *totally* "underground." While a pyramid gathers the powers of the underworld and the cosmos to a worldly focus—its point, after all, is in this world—the Receptive man or woman has little interest in worldly power for its own sake. If power comes, it will be as a by-product of immersion in the inner world, whether as an artist, teacher, healer, mystic, or psychic. Often as a result of uncanny experiences, the Receptive's self-concept is not solid or resistant. Insights well up from deeper than the personal, and the person may feel like a medium or a channel.

If you just looked out across the desert, you could easily overlook the Receptive Cube. It wasn't built to get your attention. It was sunk, like a well, in search of water, the source of life. You know without our having to pin a New Age name on it what water signifies to the soul; just think how awful it is to go through an emotional, creative, or spiritual "dry spell." That's why you can often find a Receptive Cube by the trees inclining around it, absorbing its nourishment. The Receptive person can be an oasis for others simply by virtue of tapping into that underground source.

Authenticity and thoughtful honesty are important to Receptives. If you are one, you know that to feel well, you need to stay tuned to your ever-changing inner truth. You spend many of your waking hours in introspection, and you are frustrated when you can't remember your dreams. Long heart-to-heart talks with a friend or lover are a satisfying forum for soul-searching, asking out loud the questions you're always asking yourself anyway: "What do I really think?" and "What do I really feel?" and "How can I express it precisely?" You are, in turn, an intuitive and sympathetic listener, but not an impenetrably gracious one like the Unsung Hero, who wants to hear all about what you're doing, but not what you're undergoing. The Receptive's Cube may be underground, but it's *open*. You listen from your heart, fearlessly using your own emotional experience as a basis for understanding and finding common ground.

Receptivity implies not just openness, but a certain hunger for experience, feelings, insights, intimacy. A Receptive man or woman isn't needy so much as *ready:* "Come on, give me your best shot! Bring on your play, I've got a stage." This person's inner life isn't primarily a fantasy life, like the Visionary's. It requires real input from the outside. You could call Receptives the Realists of the inner world. As Realists are in their element dealing with material and social reality, so are Receptives with emotional reality.

An architect we know, who saw white flowers falling into her cubic pool, said, "Of course—I really want to have a baby!" But her Cube was more than just Freudian shorthand for her womb. She wanted the *experiences* of pregnancy, birth, and the intense bond between mother and child. She wanted to be filled with life, not only physically, but emotionally and mentally. And, more often than not, life complies. Receptives seem to be given more than the usual share of strong experiences, even tragedies. It's as if life responds, "You really want my best shot? Okay, you asked for it!" But the Receptive usually proves equal to the challenge, rolls with the punches and is toughened, softened, deepened, seasoned by them. As a Chinese proverb has it, "The human heart rolls and tumbles until finally it becomes a human heart."

@

THE RECEPTIVE AT WORK

The Receptives we know have artistic talent, especially for composing space. They seem to be drawn to occupations like architecture, interior design, landscaping, stagecraft, art direction (graphic or cinematic), and film direction. Their awareness of interiority enables them to create spaces that, in turn, shape the dweller's or viewer's mood and state of mind. Since music, too, creates a space around the listener and seeks to re-create an inner state, it's easy to imagine a musician being Receptive, though we haven't encountered one yet. Certainly our Receptive friends are impassioned listeners.

Receptives also flourish in occupations that involve nurturing, including full-time motherhood, social work, psychotherapy, psychic counseling, all kinds of one-on-one teaching, and the healing professions. Indeed, they are apt to take on such roles with coworkers or clients even when it's not how they earn their living. We know a small-town plumber and handyman, secretly psychic, who tends to his closest clients' gardens and heartaches. Because they are drawing from deeper than the personal, Receptive people aren't easily depleted. Except in periods of personal stress and crisis (and sometimes even then), they actually seem to thrive on intense interaction and tireless giving.

It may be the Receptives among us who do the most to make the emotional desert of the workplace blossom—and not only by the way they decorate their cubicles! This is the one person at work you can always confide in,

@

THE RECEPTIVE IN LOVE

What can keep a Receptive from fulfillment, however, is loneliness. Receptives operate at a full-throttle intensity and a pitch of intimacy that not many others can comfortably handle. As T. S. Eliot drily noted, "Humankind cannot bear very much reality." Too real for most Visionaries, too "heavy" for most Realists, too personal for most Principled, and too probing for the Unsung Hero, a Receptive may burn out or scare off quite a few lovers before finally finding the rare one who can take it—"it" being constant sharing and analysis of the relationship. (A Perfectionist might like all the attention.) To Receptives, there's nothing more real or fascinating than the moment-to-moment changes in human emotions—theirs or yours. Tracking and talking out those changes (be warned, this type can talk you to death) is their way of staying on the bucking bronco of the truth, even when it's a wild ride. It's also their way of penetrating deeper into a lover's psyche, getting close.

If the very thought makes you gasp for air, beware the Receptive lover. He or she is not only out to know you through and through, but to find your deepest wounds and heal them. One thing Receptives love to do is love a damaged person back to life. They'll unerringly zero in on someone who, to the naked eye, looks like a lost cause—resigned to a loveless marriage, a lonely life, a chronic illness—and make a long and patient project of wooing them, winning their trust, astonishing them with attention, till they blossom who is genuinely interested in your inner life, not just your output. For a Receptive, work exists to support human interaction, not vice versa. Only a shortsighted manager would assume a Receptive is "wasting time" by talking with others (though as we'll see, Receptives *can* be justly accused of talking too much). His or her contribution to the company bottom line is often indirect and qualitative—a matter of intangibles like loyalty, teamwork, and morale.

For Receptives in creative and professional fields, work—its process, substance, and quality—is its own reward. Recognition or acclaim sought for its own sake would be meaningless. Unlike the Unsung Hero, though, Receptives don't need to keep the heart hidden, so they won't try to duck the radar of recognition. They may even actively seek it out for good work's sake. After all, success is another strong experience, one that can only multiply their opportunities and interactions and thicken the plot of their lives. But they will readily acknowledge that they're "doing God's work," or that their best ideas come through them, not from them. Success won't likely go to a Receptive's head, or throw her off balance. Nor can obscurity or a modest income stop him from living a rich, fulfilling, contributing life.

in spite of themselves. It's a therapeutic Pygmalion act, like what psychiatrist Claude Rains does for Bette Davis in *Now, Voyager*. (Then, of course, she goes and falls in love with Paul Henreid. That can happen.)

Note that here compassion is a subtle form of dominance. The Receptive person usually "feels like" the older, leading partner—the initiator, healer, mentor, mother—even when he or she is younger. By being the one to talk about both your feelings and their own, Receptives, like a rodeo rider, manage to stay on top. By constantly "facing" feelings, like a lion tamer, they avoid being ambushed by them. It makes you wonder whether their seeming fearlessness in love isn't really "counterphobic," like skydiving—controlling a fear by getting the jump on it, diving in.

And so, lonely Receptives have a choice: wait for someone willing to be "heavy" with them, or lighten up a little. A Receptive woman might be among the most likely to opt for single motherhood, since babies and little kids won't flee if you gaze deep into their eyes. But not all Receptives are women. A possible hunting ground might be those New Age Jungian or tantric workshops for people who want a brave new intimacy, not just company. There, instead of trying to rescue castaways and convert commitment-phobes, you might find someone who will gaze back into your eyes and call your bluff.

RECEPTIVE SEX

Many Receptives seem to believe that the unexamined sex life is not worth living. It's not so much the physical but the emotional vicissitudes of the act that have to be discussed. If the other partner wants to withdraw, talking about it is a way of holding on to contact. If only the true feelings behind the withdrawal can be unearthed, the other person will want to stay close. Right? That sounds like a woman's misconception about men, but it can go the other way, too. It's hard for a Receptive of any sex to understand that a Realist might just be satisfied and ready for what's next, a Visionary might want to drag the experience off and fantasize about it, a Principled or Perfectionist might find it all too flawed and messy, and an Unsung Hero might just think it's none of your business.

Again, though, if honesty and full disclosure is what you really want, a Receptive person isn't afraid to give it to you. These are people who can turn emotion and sex into a spiritual adventure as challenging as mountain-climbing. It takes a special kind of courage to expose oneself, naked, to the extremes of *inner* weather and to the full knowledge of a lover. The word "tantric" comes to mind again. In the movie *Bliss*, a young man, under the guidance of a tantric therapist, devotes himself to the patient penetration of his own and his troubled wife's defenses. The skinless, oceanic, infinitely gentle pleasure they attain is so exquisite, only a Receptive could stand it.

©

THE RECEPTIVE AT PLAY

Receptives play well with Expatriates, because both are perfectly happy sitting around talking, drinking endless cups of coffee. (They're apt to smoke, too. They're *oral*, of course—the very meaning of Receptivity, and the common thread that links their hunger for life to their compulsive talking.) The Receptive loves to ruminate and to analyze anything—a divorce in the family, a movie, an event in the news. Everything that is taken in must be broken down, digested, and absorbed into the inner world, and this can occupy as many hours each day as a ruminant's cud-chewing. Others may become restless to be *doing* something, but the Receptive can stay engrossed for hours in the mental activity of reexperiencing and examining an event or emotion, extracting every last bit of nourishment from it, sucking the marrow from its bones.

Of course, Receptives' hunger for experience extends to the vicarious experiences of art, especially movies, music, and theater, which offer *more* emotion, *more* life. And Receptives like to be actively engaged in creative projects, especially those that involve designing, building, or decorating something—from a kitchen cabinet to a stage set. In this respect, their play is hardly distinguishable from their work (and as parents, they really know how to jump-start their kids' creativity). When they're not making something of their own, they're happy to pitch in on a friend's project. The best way to play with a Receptive—or, in an emergency, to shut one up—is to ask for help with something along the lines of an amateur dramatic production, a community playground, or a redecorating scheme.

■

The position of your Cube tells you a lot about yourself, but there's much more still to learn. Just as in astrology your sun sign is only the beginning, and it takes a full chart to do justice to your one-of-a-kindness, in "the Cube" your individuality is pinpointed by the intersection of three variables: position, size, and (perhaps most fascinating of all) material. How big a place do you claim in the scheme of things? And what are you made of? Steel? Cloud? Ice? Bird's-eye maple? The next two chapters will complete the portrait of the main character in your life's drama.

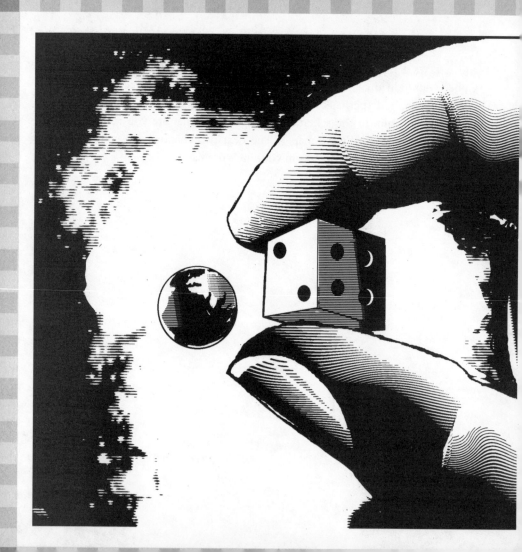

CHAPTER 11

HOW BIG?
HOW FAR?

O ne of our favorite moments in playing the Cube comes when we ask, "How big is it?" The answer is often so unexpected, and yet so *right*, that it's a struggle not to laugh out loud and make our innocent subjects self-conscious, wondering what they've just revealed about themselves. You, too, will need to keep a straight face as you learn that your nit-picking boss has quite a small Cube, or your bossy sister quite a large one.

One of the surprises of this game is discovering how well we know ourselves—how objective and accurate an eye is trained on us from within. Self-deception and wishful thinking are *conscious* activities. Deeper down, we know and accept the truth. And one of the truths we know about ourselves is this business of size.

It's not a simple equation—big Cube, big ego; small Cube, small talent. Not at all. For one thing, the material of your Cube, "the stuff you're made of," can totally reverse the message of size. (Imagine a very large Cube made of paper—a paper tiger—versus a tiny precious gem.) And then, too, people can be "large" or "small" in a number of ways. For example, most people who have small Cubes also have modest, realistic ambitions. That almost seems to be one of the meanings of a small Cube. But some people with small Cubes are gnawed by feelings of inferiority, resentment, and envy, which can drive them to back-stabbing and petty power trips. They are among the most miserable people to be and to be with, because they are fighting against the message their subconscious is sending them, wanting to be more than they are.

"Large" and "small," of course, are themselves relative terms. Larger than what? Smaller than what? Compared to the planet, the Pentagon is minuscule. What you mean by the words "large" or "small" is as revealing as your Cube's actual dimensions. We've had people say "The cube's quite large," only to learn that it's the size of a bread box. Well, yes, that's pretty large from the perspective of dice, or mice. What scale are you thinking on? That's one good measure of your ambitions, though not the only one (shininess, for instance, is another—see page 187). If a bread box–sized cube seems "large" to you, you'll most likely be content with modest achievements and lifestyle. (If your bread box is encrusted with diamonds, that's another story.)

At the other extreme is a megalomaniac like Slobodan, whose "large" Cube is longer than a marathon and as high as a jet's cruising altitude. And even *he's* a piker compared to another film director whose Cube is the size of the moon—and made of green cheese. (What *is* it with these film directors? We'll get to that.) In between are most people, who would define "large" as "significantly larger than me." For convenience, we're going to classify Cubes as "small" (less than knee-high), "medium" (within human scale), and "large" (higher than you can reach). Slobodan's, we guess, would be "extra large."

Of course, the *perceived* size of a cube in the desert also depends on its distance from the viewer. Advertising photographer Bert Stern once famously traveled all the way to Egypt to capture the image of the Great Pyramid of Giza inverted in a martini glass. It was smaller than the olive! Sometimes, when we ask "How big is the cube?" we get an interesting answer: "I'm not sure, because I don't know how far away it is." Or: "Small—but it's way off on the horizon." "You mean, if you got close to it," we say, "it might be very big?" The answer almost always is, "Yes. [pause] *Very* big."

This offers a fascinating clue to the meaning of the distance between you and your Cube (which, after all, is *you*, too). Growing up is a process of putting oneself in perspective, more or less outgrowing childish egotism (a toddler's Cube would probably fill the cosmos), and granting parity, if not priority, to the world beyond the self. The distance of your Cube, as well as its size, reflects the balance or bargain you've struck between self and world. Someone whose Cube is small gives more weight to the world than to the self. But someone whose Cube only *looks* small, because it's far away, has deferred to the demands of reality while holding on to a secret sense of importance. It's the difference between "I know I am a small person in a big world" and "I can act the part of a small person in a big world, but I know better, and if you get close to me, you will, too." This can be someone who had dreams of glory in the past—and may still hold some in reserve for the future.

People who say they can't tell how big the cube is, because they don't know how far away it is, are even more canny—or is it wise? It's as if you asked them, "How important are you?" and they shrugged and said, "Depends on your point of view." That's true, of course, but it's also strategic—a kind of cloaking device or evasive maneuver. You may find this is someone who doesn't like to be pinned down, who prefers to keep options open—definitely *not* the type to declare, like Martin Luther, "Here I stand!"

The size and distance of the Cube can have other meanings as well. Here are some of them, drawn from our trove of cubing experience. Cross-reference this information with the position and material (see the next chapter) of the Cube, and you'll have quite a complex portrait of yourself or someone you work, live, or play with.

❧

LARGE CUBES

Someone whose Cube is higher than he or she can reach has one or more of the following qualities:

Positive	Negative
confidence	egotism
self-esteem	grandiosity
generosity	self-importance
subjectivity	self-absorption
aspiration	domination
adventurousness	

The size of your Cube doesn't necessarily reflect the size of your body. People with big cubes may not be physically big at all, but they invariably "think big" in some way: They aim high, loom large, show largesse. They may have big hearts, big brains, big mouths, or big plans. They tend to be expansive (an astrologer would say Jupiterian), confident, and relatively fearless. They can also be overbearing and/or self-preoccupied. ("But enough about me. What do *you* think about me?")

If extroverted, they may naturally dominate or lead, both at home and at work (see the relative size of the Ladder for more clues); if introverted, they have a big and busy inner life. A large part of their picture of the world is occupied by their subjectivity. That is, they're at least as interested in their own thoughts, feelings, plans, and memories as they are in the evening news, history, politics, or sociology. A large Cube can be helpful for ego accomplishment, as it corresponds to that relative obliviousness to the opinions of others and the law of averages that is often necessary for success.

In our experience (though there are exceptions), people in the creative arts tend to have larger Cubes than those working or living within a "system"—be it business, a profession, a trade, or a religious tradition. That fits with the inner life, individualism, ego, and daring it takes to create these days. But of all creative people, film directors take the prize for most outlandishly outsized Cubes. We asked ourselves why: Are they raving egomaniacs? Dictators? Perhaps they have to be a little of both to do what they do. But more to the point, directors don't inhabit the world—they create one. And to oversee that world from top to bottom and beginning to end, like gods, they have to be bigger than their creations. A film director's unique perspective is illustrated by Slobodan's Cube: It's twenty-six miles on a side, yet to him it's just a tiny black square—because he's seeing it from orbit!

SMALL CUBES

Someone whose Cube is smaller than knee-high will show one or more of these traits:

Positive	Negative
humility	timidity
selflessness	undervaluing of self
objectivity	literal-mindedness
realism	conventionality
intimacy	concealment
preciousness (as of stone or metal)	pettiness

Smallness doesn't necessarily equate with modesty or insignificance. Diamonds and other precious things are small. They pack a concentrated value and power that belies their dimensions. So it's especially important to take note of the material of a small Cube. Someone who describes it as "a gold brick" or "a fist-sized diamond radiating light" doesn't exactly undervalue him- or herself. You can measure this one's self-esteem in karats, or carats.

Small Cubes made of more ordinary materials *usually* belong, as we've said, to people who give more weight to the world than to the self. They have no illusions about their own importance in the larger scheme of things—a realism that prevents them from hatching grand schemes—and they generally find the world outside them more real, rich, and fascinating than their inner world. They tend to be more interested in facts than feelings, and to take the events of news and history at face value. They often have a strong sense of community responsibility and service to others. They have not read *Looking Out for No. 1.*

People with small Cubes tend to be content working as a small cog within a large system. Perhaps that's why lawyers so consistently have small Cubes (although flamboyant celebrity lawyers are a likely exception). When someone with a small Cube achieves success, it is usually through hard work, responsibility, and meticulous attention to detail rather than swashbuckling charisma. But beware of the boss or bureaucrat with a small Cube. This can be a petty tyrant who lords it over his or her tiny kingdom by brandishing the rule book. There are petty tyrants in families, too: the arbitrary parent, the sniping spouse, the prissy, tattletale sibling. When a small, hard Cube is paired with a sore, swollen ego, the shoe pinches, and the person is always cranky.

A couple of special cases: When someone says the Cube is "small enough to hold in your hand," grab his or her hand and don't let go. You've found someone who doesn't fear intimacy; on the contrary, this is a warm person with a real gift for emotional closeness. And having a very small Cube can sometimes be a strategy for escaping attention (see the Realist subtype we call "Hiding Out," page 85). People can have any number of reasons for doing this, ranging from the innocuous (not wanting to be bothered) to the sinister (not wanting to get caught). Check it out.

©

MEDIUM CUBES

Someone whose Cube is within human scale (from knee height to as high as you can reach) has one or more of the following characteristics:

Positive	Negative
balance	averageness
warmth	health or body image problems
modesty	
self-respect	
humanism	

People with medium-sized Cubes strike a fairly even balance between self and world, subjectivity and objectivity, ego and modesty. The fact that their sense of self is roughly the size of their physical self suggests that they are at peace with who they are, at ease in their own skins. But not always: It can also signal an identification with the body, and that, strangely, is often the result of physical problems. Healthy people feel *free* of the body, while nothing brings you back to your actual boundaries and limitations like an illness or allergy (unless it's living in Los Angeles, where you *are* your body. Unless you're your money). Petite young women often seem to have Cubes toward the small end of human scale, perhaps because their physical vulnerability is never far from their awareness.

Cubes that take their dimensions from the human body recall Leonardo da Vinci's classic drawing of a naked man measuring a circle with his extended arms and legs, and the Renaissance epigram that went with it: "Man is the measure of all things." That idea, in turn, was taken from the Greeks, who modeled their temple columns on the proportions of the human form. In art and architecture, human scale is associated with humanism and democracy, which created a middle ground of face-to-face relationships and individual sovereignty in between mass anonymity and the tyrant's cult of personality. Today, one can easily feel lost in the vastness of society and its institutions (the little Cube), or can overcompensate by becoming a real or fantasy celebrity (the big Cube). People with medium Cubes succeed in avoiding both extremes, being content to matter to a human-scale community of family, friends, and peers.

If a particular part of the body is used to define the Cube's size—"It's knee-high," "It comes up to my heart," "It's just over my head"—take that as a meaningful message and try to decode it. What does that part of the body signify traditionally? What does it mean to you personally? What's the first association that comes to mind? (Knees, for instance, are traditionally associated with humility. But a modest man we know whose Cube is knee-high also has arthritis that he feels has "cut him off at the knees.") A twenty-six-year-old martial artist and aspiring writer told us, "If I stretch, I can just reach the top [of the cube]"—which translates as "the best of me," "my full potential." This young man believes he has what it takes to achieve any goal he sets for himself. Actress Jasmine Guy and a male doctor friend of ours in Florida both described their Cube's size by saying, "I can put my arms around it"—a sure sign of someone warm, caring, and passionate.

◉

NEAR CUBES, FAR CUBES

Regardless of whether the gap is large or small, the separation between you, the viewer, and your self, the Cube, is one of the lingering mysteries of the game. This separation is almost universal; very rarely does someone say, "I'm inside the cube." (What people more often do say is, "It's big enough for me to get inside it.")

One clue to the mystery may be found in Buddhist insight meditation, or Vipassana, in which meditators practice observing themselves: their breath, their physical sensations, their thoughts. The aim is to create a gap, to make people aware that their observing consciousness is separate and distinct from their body and personality. The Cube shows that that perspective is already in us naturally: We *know* we're not only our body and personality. That's why we are looking at our Cube across a distance that varies, perhaps, with how impulsive or reflective we are.

At the beginning of this chapter, we described your Cube's distance from you as "perspective on yourself." But there seems to be a point of diminishing returns: When the Cube is *very* far away, it can also mean *estrangement* from yourself—a lack of self-knowledge or an avoidance of introspection. The result can be estrangement from others as well.

A friend of ours cubed her grandmother, a rather unhappy and unpleasant woman. Her Cube, the grandmother said, was tiny, hard, black, and so far away she had no idea what it was made of. According to our friend, her grandmother was a bright and gifted woman who had followed the conventional path for women of her generation—marriage and children—even though education and art would have suited her better. Her Cube had dwindled away from lack of attention, and had withdrawn into a hard and bitter isolation. This is a cautionary tale. Perhaps playing the Cube when we're still young can help to save us from such a fate.

On the other hand, if the Cube is *very* close, we may have little or no perspective on ourselves, and lack the capacity for self-observation that leads to both self-understanding and self-control. We may be naively identified with our personality and emotions, and that's finally as limiting as being out of touch with them. Short of those extremes, each of us strikes a characteristic balance between the qualities of closeness and distance.

Which of these resonate for you?

IMPULSIVITY VS. DELIBERATION

A Far Cube
deliberates before acting
watches himself/herself
rational self-control
self-denial

A Near Cube
spontaneous
emotional
impulsive
quick-tempered

PERSONAL SPACE.
[SEE ALSO THE LADDER.]

A Far Cube
independent
standoffish
likes solitude
needs lots of space

A Near Cube
intimate, cozy
sociable
likes company
"Life is with people."

ABSTRACT VS. CONCRETE THINKING

A Far Cube
abstract
big-picture oriented
visual ("Can I get an overview of it?")

A Near Cube
concrete
detail-oriented
tactile ("Can I get my hands on it?")

TIME AND SPACE HORIZONS

A Far Cube	**A Near Cube**
takes the long view	reacts to the immediate
memory and planning	lives in the present
focus: the wide world	focus: what's right here

■

Whatever the distance between you and your Cube, you're about to close that gap by *becoming* your Cube. To find out "what you're made of," it's not enough just to look. You need to shift from visualization to the fuller technique of "imaging," which includes feeling. What you know about your Cube with the "distance sense" of your mind's eye will now be completed by the intimacy of touch and of *proprioception,* or "sensing self." You'll explore the Cube from within as if it were your own body, because in a sense it is: the "body" of your soul.

CHAPTER 12

WHAT'S
IT MADE OF?

Now comes the most fascinating, sensuous, and subtle part of decoding your Cube: its material. Here's where you really get to feel the flesh of your spirit, the substance of your soul. And here's also where you get to find out something you really didn't know about your mate, your colleague, or your mom.

When you learn the position and size of someone's Cube, you'll often react with recognition: "Yeah, that's the person I know." You feel you could almost have guessed that your friend was a ten-foot Perfectionist or a down-to-earth toaster. But the Cube's material unveils a secret and a mystery. There's no way you could have predicted it, and no other way you could have discovered it. You're learning how that person *feels* to himself or herself—almost how it feels to *be* him or her. It is always unexpected, often touching, and occasionally chilling (look out for those non-melting ice cubes!). And this mysterious hit of someone else's subjectivity comes in a wordless language that instantaneously delivers a huge amount of information to your intuition. If a picture is worth a thousand words, surely a touch is worth thousands more—heft, density, texture, temperature, a soul's whole signature in a single flash.

❂

YOUR SOULPRINT

It's the material, too, that makes each Cube truly one of a kind. We like to call the Cube a "soulprint" because if ever there was proof that our souls are as unique as our genes, faces, and fingerprints, it's the nearly infinite variation in the stuff we imagine ourselves to be made of. (Yep, we've cubed identical twins. And their cubes, while strikingly similar—often very close in size and color—also show distinct differences. For example, two twenty-two-year-old French Canadian girls we know both have Cubes of a deep sky blue, about six feet tall. But one is all walls with an open center, and the other is all interior with no walls! In addition, one twin is Principled—her Cube is up on a hill—while the other is a Realist.)

There's no way to list or describe *all* the materials we've heard of, and even if we could, we'd hear a new one tomorrow. Cubes are made of every liquid, solid, gaseous, animal, vegetable, and mineral substance you can think of, and some that you can't. Some people find no existing material that feels right, so they invent one. An Expatriate Israeli artist's Cube (and Ladder, too) is molded of a translucent golden resin. A Perfectionist theater director and teacher says her Cube's surface is woven, like plaid fabric, only hard. A six-foot, six-inch gastroenterologist and avant-garde art collector has a small, hovering cube of insubstantial blue shimmer.

As for more familiar materials, here's a very partial list, just to give you an idea: cloud, sponge, marble, rubber, cheese, steel, ice, paper, rock, light, plastic, honey, adobe, air, aluminum, golf ball, flesh, diamond, wood, smoke, silver, canvas, glass, ocean water, terra cotta, titanium, and . . . *frozen pink lemonade!* And within many of these are myriad fine shadings and variations: Think about all the different *kinds* of cloud, glass, rock, wood, plastic, and steel.

How can we impose any order on this glorious mélange? And how can *we* say with any authority what a material means to the person who's "made of" it? Nothing about your Cube is more inward or intimate; your own associations will be your best guide. Even so, some identifiable patterns have emerged. We'll tell you what we know. But since we can cover only a fraction of all possible materials, here are five questions which, like a chemist's assays, should coax any substance to yield up its essence:

Is it soft or hard? Is this someone who "gives" when pushed, yields and accommodates, likes making others comfortable? A "soft touch"—nurturing, forgiving, adaptable? Or is this person firm, definite, maybe even stubborn, set in his/her opinions and ways?

On the far side of softness is *insubstantiality:* Cubes of air, light, shadow, space, cloud, or smoke that you could put your hand right through. (See, for instance, Gloria Steinem's Cube, described on page 122.) These people may lack clear boundaries and may be easily overrun by the demands of others; they may be somewhat disembodied and intellectual; or else there's something elusive or illusory—miragelike—about them. (Where there's smoke, there may be deliberate mystification—not to mention fire.)

Is it solid or hollow? Hollow cubes may be sad and empty, but more often they're just open, with inner space available to "take in" and "entertain" things. So, unless there's a lot going on inside the Cube, hollowness usually indicates openness to suggestion, interest in the outside world. A dense, solid Cube is like a computer with a full memory: This person has a jam-packed inner life and a full agenda.

Is it light or heavy? How seriously does this person take life? Is she or he more earnest and weighty, or playful and whimsical—here to have fun? Clearly, this is a continuum. (Note that, since the laws of physics here yield to the laws of dream, a Cube can be very heavy and still be floating, "in the Visionary position." Note also that a solid Cube outweighs a hollow one of the same material and size—and it's true, introverted people *do* tend to be more serious.)

Is it shiny or matte? The deep mind has let us know in no uncertain terms that "shiny" means "ambitious." Whether of highly polished stone, glass, metal, or plastic, a Cube that reflects back blinding light belongs to someone who absolutely *has* to shine. (Actress Jasmine Guy and mega-bestseller publisher Judith Regan, for example.) *Lovers' alert: This person will never sacrifice ambition for a relationship, and will, if you force the issue, do the opposite.* As a result, this is someone who knows all too well that it's lonely at the top *and* on the way there—yet that is where she or he must go. People with matte cubes are not so driven to dazzle, nor are they as "polished" or "slick."

Is it transparent, translucent, or opaque? Cubes you can see into and through often indicate candor, full disclosure, nothing to hide—in extreme cases, even a touch of exhibitionism. (Interestingly, they very often belong to people who've had therapy.) A clear Cube may also represent clear thinking, or an undistorted view of reality. People with opaque Cubes guard their privacy, are slow to reveal themselves, or have secrets. (Those with shiny Cubes, however, may "let it all shine out," using aspects of the private self as grist for their public performance.) A translucent material that lets diffuse light glow through it seems to characterize someone who is attractively mysterious, who doesn't reveal all, but *does* show emotion.

THE STUFF YOU'RE MADE OF

Now to the lowdown on some specific materials, as well as special features (such as edges or borders) and "ready-made" Cubes (like Rubik's). We've provided extra detail on the ones we know the most about.

Note that, unlike position and size, the Cube's material rarely gives clues to the kind of job, profession, or work role a person will do best in. Rather, the material indicates the kind of person he or she will be in any work situation—and any love situation. The stuff you're made of represents your "consistency" in both senses of the word. It's both "the feel of you" and the way you take that with you wherever you go. When we talk about stone, metal, plastic, glass, and ice, you'll see how a single such "consistency" can express itself both positively and negatively across the spectrum of work, love, and play. (As always, take our suggestions as a starting point, not the last word. Add and subtract qualities from those we list based on your "feel for" the person you're cubing.)

Air, space ▪ **Key word: merging**. Someone with permeable or nearly nonexistent boundaries. In our experience this kind of Cube is chosen more often—but not exclusively—by women. (See "insubstantiality," above.)

Black slab from 2001 ▪ **Key word: transformer**. Someone whose ideas or inventions advance human evolution.

Castle, fortress ▪ **Key word: guarded**. Hard to reach, cautious, slow to trust. May have been traumatized in the past. Or, saving herself/himself for the right person.

Clay, ceramic, terra cotta ▪ **Key word: permeable**. Earthy, cool, sensitive to outside influences.

Cloud ▪ **Key word: purity**. Somewhat disembodied, this person floats above, out of reach of, and unsullied by ordinary reality.

Crystal ▪ **Key word: spiritual**—and *not* necessarily New Age. We've heard this used as a spontaneous pun for "Christian."

Diamond ▪ **Key word: illumination**. A brilliantly clear, firm, incisive mind and character. Someone who sheds light on things, cuts through murk and muddle, and is quietly confident of his or her own value.

Dice ▪ **Key word: gambler**. A risk-taker in life or business; lucky.

Drawing (a line drawing of a cube): ▪ **Key word: intellectualization**. Someone who thinks abstractly, or filters life and emotion through the mind.

Edges ▪ **Key word: boundaries**. If the Cube's edges are marked with dark lines or bound by a different material, the person guards against violations of privacy and others' intrusions or demands.

Fabric (note type of fabric) ▪ **Key word: domestic**. Also, sensuous; "woven" of many influences.

Food ▪ **Key word: appetites**. An edible Cube indicates you are sensual, a lover of good food, or hungry (dieting, perhaps?). We can also imagine this Cube accompanying an eating disorder, though it's a variation we haven't seen.

▪ GLASS ▪

Mottoes: *"What you see is what you get," "Don't throw stones"*
Key words: *open, candid, factual, fragile*

	Positive	Negative
In love	communicative self-revealing	indiscreet easily hurt
At work	honest, trustworthy, clear, sees things as they are	takes things personally mixes professional and emotional life
At play	curious eager to learn	accident-prone

NOTE: *See "solid or hollow" and "transparent or translucent" above.*

VARIATIONS

Shatterproof Glass adds toughness to the candor.

Mirror can suggest:
1. people-pleasing, adapting to others
2. realism (reflecting the world as it is)
3. visual orientation ("I am a camera")

Stained Glass shows religious faith or artistic inclinations.

Colored Glass shows imagination, artistic talent, or wishful thinking.

House ▪ **Key word: sheltering**. Often the Cube of someone in real estate or architecture. And/or a nurturer and protector of others; family-centered.

▪ ICE ▪

Mottoes: *"But I was cool," "Cold, cold heart"*
Key words: *self-possessed, poised, resourceful, calm in crisis*

	Melting a Little	Non-melting
In love	responsive, emotional,	very self-controlled

	Melting a Little	Non-melting
	sexual, nurturing	withholding
	discusses differences calmly	can be manipulative
At work	clear-thinking	calculating, power-seeker
	keeps his/her head under stress	tough negotiator
	a superb strategist	
At play	unafraid	"extreme,"
	refreshing company	a daredevil

NOTE: *If your ice Cube is **melting away** in the desert heat, you've lost your cool! You're either madly in love, or falling apart under stress or grief.*

Jewel, Jeweled ■ Key word: **precious**. Can also be a pun for "Jewish."

■ METAL ■

Mottoes: *"I can take it," "Been through the fire"*
Key words: *tough, bright, tested, indestructible, impenetrable*

	Positive	Negative
In love	stands by you in trouble	doesn't want to need you
	slow to give up	slow to open up

At work	can stand stress	disillusioned, cynical
	persevering	can sell out to survive
At play	adventurous	reckless
	"no fear"	sensation-seeking

NOTES: *This person has emerged stronger from hardship, trouble, or tragedy. May be a pun for "mettle." See also "solid or hollow" and "shiny or matte" in previous sections.*

VARIATIONS

Precious metals are less about toughness than a secure sense of one's own value; high self-esteem.

Gold was someone's adored child; may be narcissistic or self-indulgent.

Silver is self-esteem hard-won through spiritual quest.
(If ordinary metals or plastic are described as gold- or silver-*colored*, combine these meanings with those of the actual material.)

Aluminum (usually a hollow Cube) suggests lightweight toughness, wanderlust, pragmatism, and cynicism (a self-protective shell).

Steel (usually a solid Cube) is introverted, impenetrable, and almost indestructible. You've had to "steel" yourself, and you've done it so well that now it would take tremendous heat to melt you.

Iron is primitive, powerful, and somber.

Copper is sexy—warm, soft, electric, temperamental.

Brass is brash, bright, attention-getting, authoritative ("top brass"), confrontational.

Titanium is ahead of its time, a futuristic thinker, at once ultra-tough and sensitive (thin-skinned).

Palace ▪ **Key word: entitlement.** High self-regard; feels he or she deserves "royal treatment."

▪ PLASTIC ▪

Mottoes: *"Salt of the earth," "Working-class hero"*
Key words: *unpretentious, blue-collar, honest, traditional, democratic*

	Positive	Negative
In love	old-fashioned	old-fashioned
	(protective/nurturing)	(sexist)

	family- and home-centered working partnership	possessive domestic battles
At work	hard-working takes pride in doing any job well	materialistic goals a dying breed
At play	good fun hospitable, generous, convivial	conventional (cards, golf) party animal

NOTES: *People with plastic Cubes invariably wince when told, "The cube is you," because consciously we think "plastic" means "cheap and fake." But it turns out that to the deep mind it means quite the opposite. It's the reliable, honest material, without pretensions, that we use for basic tasks every day—what "wood" or "iron" would have meant to an earlier time. If not actually working-class, the person will come from farm, small-town, or urban blue-collar roots.*

VARIATIONS

Plexiglass or Lucite shares the candor and toughness of shatterproof glass (above). A rainbow shimmer adds a touch of creativity, flirtation, or illusion.

Colors: A bank officer of Sicilian origin had a plastic Cube "the color of old blood"—just like the shields on his family coat of arms. What are your personal associations with the color of *your* Cube? They may or may not jibe with these common associations:

> *Red* passion, hot energy, anger, warmth
> *Green* hope, life, nature, money
> *Blue* spirituality, serenity, cool energy, sadness
> *Purple* royalty, deep passions, mourning
> *Yellow* cheerfulness, brightness, eccentricity
> *Pink* feminity, warmth
> *Brown* earthiness, warmth, conventionality
> *Black* mystery
> *White* purity
> *Multicolored* of many interests or moods

Formica: upwardly mobile plastic; attempting to disguise class origins.

Rubber ▪ Key words: bounce, humor. The comeback kid. Resilient, "bounces back" from setbacks; energetic, playful, funny.

Rubik's Cube ▪ Key word: ingenuity. Versatile, clever; enjoys solving conundrums or matching wits.

Smoke ▪ Key word: mystery. Seductive and elusive. Can't be grasped or pinned down. Hidden fire.

Spaceship ▪ **Key word: stranger**. Feels out of place in his/her present environment. May be an immigrant, or just "different."

▪ STONE ▪

Mottoes: *"I am a rock," "We shall not be moved"*
Key words: *substantial, reliable, principled, stubborn, conservative*

	Positive	**Negative**
In love	loyal, devoted, dependable a lifetime partner	obsessive, can't let go
At work	dogged, thorough, steady someone you can count on	slow to adapt to change self-willed, always knows better
At play	patient, supportive	habit-bound, in a rut

NOTES: *Is the stone—and the person—rough or smooth (indicates degree of refinement, "finish," suavity)? Does the Cube blend into the desert, or stand out? (Is this person "in his/her element" or out of place? Or, does he/she prefer to keep a high or a low profile?) Colors have personal connotations, but commonly, black = mystery; red = warmth; gray = conservatism, age, or resignation.*

VARIATIONS

Marble adds a touch of class and elegance. This person likes working with creative people.

Stone Blocks seem to be associated with piecework. A freelance journalist and a jeweler are among those we've cubed whose Cubes—like their work—are built of "pieces."

Water ▪ **Key word: emotional**. Deep-feeling, intuitive.

Wood, Beautifully finished: ▪ **Key word: cultured**. Refined, literate, sensitive.

Wood, raw or painted: ▪ **Key word: countercultural.** Funky, "natural," creative. (For colors, see page 195.)

▪

Position. Size. Material. Combined, these "three dimensions" define the uniqueness of your Cube, or any other Cube you seek to understand. Whenever you encounter a new Cube, find the closest match to its position, size, and material in the preceding chapters, and read our descriptions (the way you'd read about someone's sun, moon, and rising signs for a fuller astrological analysis). "Triangulating" these three will put you within range of an accurate character portrait.

Then the *real* fun begins. The refinements and finishing touches to that portrait must be filled in by your knowledge of that person, or better yet, *by* that person. We can't say it too many times: Our interpretation is only a starting point. The subtlest secrets of a Cube will reveal themselves only to and through the one whose Cube it is.

Perhaps the ultimate secret of your Cube, however, is beyond words, and communicates directly, the way music and abstract art do. The Cube you see in the desert is, more than a picture, *a sculpture of a feeling*—the feeling of being you. It's an enigmatic emblem of your individuality, one that holds many messages and lessons for you, yet is never emptied of meaning, or of mystery. It's also a helpful ambassador to others—since your Cube often explains you better (without words) than you could have yourself!

Sharing your complete Cube vision is the next step: It gives the people close to you a peek into your private world, including their place in it. Your Cube isn't an inanimate object; it's a chunk of pure subjectivity turned into substance, a "body" for your soul. Like every living being, it has a force field that extends well beyond it and organizes the world around it. The Cube is you, but it's how you position the Ladder, Horse, Storm, and Flowers that shows how you shape your own world. Since you bring your world invisibly with you into relationships and the workplace, and so does everyone else, the Cube, by making the invisible visible, can help us be safer, more gracious guests in each other's realities.

Having discovered the Cube's inherent qualities, we move on, now, to its interactive qualities: independence, closeness, possessiveness, dominance, dependency, nurturance, leadership, and love.

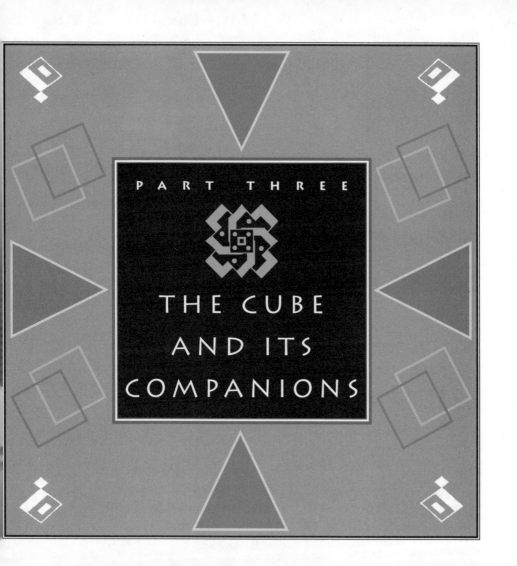

PART THREE

THE CUBE
AND ITS
COMPANIONS

SECRETS
OF THE LADDER

@

The Ladder stands for all the important people in your life with whom you aren't intimately physical. The wise ones who devised this game found a wonderfully visceral way to express the difference between these two kinds of relationships—the erotic (in a broader sense than just sexual) and the platonic. Those people who are vitally linked to you through your body—your lover and your children—appear in the desert as living things, volatile and vulnerable, while the people linked to you by friendship or work show up as a familiar and trusty *object*, cool, firm, and stable. Sometimes the Ladder also stands for your family of origin, a set of once-volcanic relationships that often cool to the solid state of friendship in adulthood.

A ladder's prosaic usefulness is a good, sturdy metaphor for our practical interdependence with others, both in private life and at work. It reminds us that we cannot rise in this world without each other's help and support. But a ladder is also a spiritual symbol—think of Jacob's Ladder in the Bible, with the angels traveling up and down. There's also a ladder in Buddhism, with seven rainbow rungs representing the stages to enlightenment. Most provocatively of all, the Sufis, who refer to themselves simply as "we friends," have spoken of the lifesaving properties of ladders as an oblique way of talking about what they do.

"[H]ow can one method [of spiritual training or transformation] be as good as another?" a questioner asked the Afghan Sufi Idries Shah. Shah answered (in his book *Learning How to Learn*):

"If a house is on fire, two ladders may be propped against one window. Both lead to the ground. The different colours of the paint on them may obscure the fact that they are ladders."

"But how do we know that either is a ladder?" the questioner persisted.

"You know by learning to recognise a ladder when you see one. . . . "

"Are some ladders too short?" the questioner wanted to know.

"Ladders are in all conditions: new, old, rotten, short, long, blue, green, weak, strong, available, in use elsewhere, and all the rest of the possibilities." What matters, Shah said, is "to conceive that the house is on fire. If you can do so without becoming obsessed or irrational about it . . . you may get out. But while you are full of hope or fear, of sentiment or desire for . . . recognition, you will not be able to use a ladder, [and] you may not be able to recognise one . . . "

This suggests that the Cube may once have been administered as a test of one's readiness to make spiritual progress and to recognize and use *true* Friends, the kind who can guide you safely out of the emergency of ignorance. Today, in using the Cube for entertainment and a more everyday brand of psychological insight, we may be like children using a navigational gyroscope to play spin-the-top. Of course, the wonder of such ancient devices is that they *can* be used and enjoyed on so many different levels. And in our "ordinary" friendships, there *does* linger a faint echo (sometimes not so faint) of that other kind of Friend and guide. The fashionably jaundiced Sartre may have declared that "Hell is other people," but the wisdom of the Cube says otherwise—it says other people are, at least potentially, our stairway to heaven. Both by inspiring our love and by trying our patience, they reveal us to ourselves—and lead us beyond the four walls of our own Cube.

Where you *put* your Ladder, and the type and size of ladder you choose, is highly individual and revealing. It shows, at a glance, something about the *kind* of people you attract and interact with; the approximate *number* who people your personal world—how many you can comfortably relate to and not go into overload; whether your bond with them is more practical or sentimental; whether you tend to lead or follow, dominate or defer—or seek out your equals; and just how close or free, intimate or independent you prefer to be. We differ dramatically in all these ways, and the Ladder can embody them all with eerie accuracy. It's shorthand for your entire style of "platonic" relating.

Here's an example. Annie's short, smooth-sanded white-pine ladder, with three or four rungs, floats in front of her floating steel Cube but doesn't touch it. She's married to Jacques, who, in total contrast, has a metal fire-engine ladder with endless extensions that shoot from his Cube up into the sky and out of sight. Do opposites attract or what? Jacques is, in fact, much more sociable; he has squadrons of friends and is often calling them or cooking them dinner. As an actor, he has a genius for making new friends of the people he works with. Annie is more introverted, and gets together with her few close friends (whom she views as gentler fellow Visionaries) less often; as a freelance writer, too, she is on her own, and has minimal contact with just a few people. But she values the people in her life—even in her professional life—for reasons of kinship and affection first (the wooden Ladder), while Jacques, as a prison-camp survivor, puts more emphasis on the *practical* benefits of friendship (the metal Ladder). A friend once literally saved his life (what else are fire-engine ladders for?), numerous advantages have come to him through friendship, and he believes friends will be his route to ultimate success.

It's fascinating to see how different people balance platonic and erotic relationships, treat them very much alike, or give one priority over the other. A Lone Crusader Hollywood agent we cubed had his Flowers growing right around his Cube on top of its pedestal, while his Horse (a unicorn) protectively circled them. His Ladder, however, was well outside that magic circle, broken, bent, and blackened. He says it's true—he has no real friends in "the business," only relationships blighted by betrayal. He trusts no one outside his family. At the other extreme are people who prop their Ladder against the Cube, but put their Horse and Flowers off at a distance. That pattern can indicate a divorced person who gets solace from work and friends—or a workaholic who dodges intimacy by spending more time with the "office family" than the one at home.

The way the Cube and its companions are arranged in the desert can give you an almost absurdly literal picture of how much closeness, support, and "space" a person needs. Ladder, Horse, and Flowers may *all* be clustered close to the Cube—the sign of an involved, affectionate "people person." Two of the elements may be paired, and therefore associated: when the Horse is near the Ladder (or tied to it), for instance, it generally means you regard your lover as your friend. Or, the elements may *all* have space between them—indicating a wish to control the level of involvement, guard one's autonomy, and perhaps keep different relationships distinct and apart. Novelist Douglas Coupland (*Generation X, Microserfs*), whom we cubed for our first book, described his Cube, Ladder, and Horse as "arranged sort of like stones in a Japanese garden. And those spatial relationships are not haphazard. It's all very well thought out."

Just to show you that the pun really *is* mightier than the word, Coupland described his lying-down Ladder as "just a generic household ladder, wood. It's the type that if you want to make it longer you can extend it. So if you want to go to about the third or fourth story, you can do it." At the time we cubed him, Coupland had published three of his generational tales and had a fourth one in the works—*literally* stretching his friendships (which, we can conjecture, provided at least some source material) "to the fourth story"! Coupland also described taking novelistic liberties with his rather nondescript Ladder, sticking it upright in the sand "to make it more sculpturally interesting." When we told him what the Ladder meant, he was suddenly stricken with a stab of novelist's guilt: "Oh, no! I'm not nice enough to my *friends!*"

As we've said, the Cube just shows you your life in a surrealistic mirror; it's up to you what, if anything, to do about it. Coupland's insight may have made him more appreciative of his friends—or just more rueful about the heartlessness that goes into heartfelt art. Seeing her detached, floating Ladder *did* provoke Annie to admit she needs her friends and resolve to stay in better touch with them

In the realm of work, it's especially well worth acting on what you learn from the placement of the Ladder—your own, an employee's, or a colleague's. You'll usually find that people have naturally gravitated to a role that corresponds to the placement of their Ladder, as well as the position of their Cube. But when someone is unhappy or ineffective in a job, cubing them will often reveal a misfit between the job's requirements and the person's inner pattern. Someone whose Ladder is leaning against the Cube may struggle in vain as a solo entrepreneur; she or he at least needs a partner. A person whose Ladder stands off at a distance from the Cube will suffer more than most in a steno pool or cubicle; quitting to become a traveling sales rep, freelancer, or consultant will transform his or her life. Someone whose Cube is much taller than the Ladder will chafe as a subordinate and needs to be given responsibility. You'll find many more examples in the following guide.

❧

MATERIAL

"The stuff your Ladder's made of" reveals much about the way you choose, regard, and relate to the people closest to you. Before we look into the meanings of specific materials, notice the contrast or similarity between your Ladder and Cube.

Compared to the Cube, is the Ladder made of the same or similar material? Or is it totally different?

When Cube and Ladder are *both* made of metal, wood, or any other material, it suggests you're most comfortable with people who are like you in some fundamental way—whether it's social background, life experiences, interests, religious beliefs, or political opinions. You've probably stayed friends with the people you grew up or went to school with. You may prefer living in a relatively homogeneous community. And in your work environment, too, you tend to gravitate to "birds of a feather"—people who either come from similar backgrounds, or work in related professional fields or at the same level of the company. Jacques' Cube is titanium and his Ladder is metal, too: He feels that only people with a degree of streetwise, survivor toughness can truly understand him. A twenty-six-year-old Web master, whose Cube is (naturally) a supercomputer and who works *and* plays mostly with fellow tech heads, has an intricately jointed metal Ladder that's about as high-tech as ladders get. If likeness of the Cube and Ladder is really important to you, it won't matter *what* your Cube is made of—you'll invent a glass ladder if you have to. We've seen 'em.

If your Ladder is made of a very different material than your Cube, the next question for you is: Just *how* is it different? Is the Ladder harder? Softer? Stronger? More fragile? Plainer? More ornate? This shows not only the kind of people you like to have around you, but also how you *perceive* them in comparison with yourself. It's at least as revealing of the role you cast *yourself* in—the tougher, or plainer, or brighter one—as it is of your companions. The Ladder is your friends and coworkers as seen through *your* eyes and *your* needs. It may or may not correspond to the way they see themselves. For instance, you may need to perceive those around you as stronger or softer than *they* think they are.

You may have a hunch that your Ladder particularly represents one person—your best friend, a close coworker, a mentor or protégé. Then it's fun to compare your Ladder with that person's Cube, and vice versa. Here's an example from our personal experience of how Cubes and Ladders can shed light on the intricacies of a relationship:

Annie's short, smooth-sanded but unfinished white-pine ladder looks like the ones in Indian pueblos. Her close friend, a fellow writer, happens to be short and blond. She's also part Mexican Indian, and saw her own Cube as unglazed terra cotta. Both elegantly simple, natural, Southwestern materials. But then their perceptions diverge.

Annie's Ladder, like her Cube, is floating; she'd like to think of her friend as a fellow Visionary. Her friend knows better: That terra cotta Cube is firmly down to earth. (She *does* have much more financial sense.) And it keeps company with a paint-spattered Ladder, a sure sign of creative collaboration. Indeed, she incorporates close friends' feedback into her work, while Annie, the compulsively self-reliant type (nothing touches *her* Cube), would like to return the compliment but can't.

Now on to the most common materials.

Wood ▪ **Key word: sentiment**. Because wood still resonates with its life as a tree, a wooden Ladder, while not quite as alive in the desert as your Horse or Flowers, is not quite an inanimate object, either. Wood is a kindred, aesthetically appealing material that is warm to the touch and that is *changed* by our touch, becoming darkened and worn in ways that make it, not ugly, but familiar and dear. (Of course it may sometimes look dull and ordinary, a case of familiarity breeding contempt.) Old and well-used is somehow the proper condition of a wooden ladder, like the one in your grandfather's garage. Such ladders are closely bound up with family, memory, and continuity—as evocative as Proust's madeleine. To have a brand-new wooden ladder is to admire its fresh, clean grain, but also to look forward to using it for many years and making it ours.

It follows that the person whose Ladder is wood likes to form lasting, irreplaceable relationships whose primary basis is affection, loyalty, familiarity, and warmth. Friends and close coworkers are "family." They may certainly *also* be relied on for help, cooperation, support, and advancement—look at the position of the Ladder to see—but that comes second. The bond itself comes first.

Everything has its downside, and the organic warmth of wood brings with it the inevitable drawback of perishability. Relationships that are emotional and irreplaceable put you at certain risk for the pain of loss (though that prospect may seem distant if your wooden Ladder is new). You form personal attachments to the people you work with that will make reassignment or changing jobs a wrenching experience. You may never fully get over the loss of an important friend, whether to betrayal, quarrel, relocation, illness, or death. Not that everyone doesn't feel these things, but you take them most to heart; people with aluminum Ladders, for instance, protect themselves by investing less emotionally.

It's highly significant that **rickety, wobbly** ladders (unreliable or ailing people), **lying-down** ladders (companionable but unhelpful people), and ladders with **broken or missing rungs** (usually people close to you who've died) are almost always made of wood. We've even cubed a woman whose Ladder was made of balsa wood—lightweight and utterly useless for support! Wood is a kind of flesh, and the flesh is weak. People who choose and bond with their associates on the basis of emotion don't always make pragmatic choices. In fact, their choices may be downright quixotic. You love "your people" for who they are, with all their flaws; you didn't pick them for strength, strategic alliance, or survival value in a foxhole. And so they may let you down, be a drag on you, or cause you grief with their self-destructiveness. A wooden ladder means both that "your people" are more vulnerable to such human weaknesses, and that *you* are more vulnerable to the sadness of their breakage and decay. But better to have loved and lost . . .

Look for some (not necessarily all) of these qualities in the person whose Ladder is wood:

	Positive	**Negative**
Among friends	warm	easily hurt
	loyal	a sucker for hard-luck stories
	comfortable	overly tolerant
At work	brings heart to work	too undemanding
	company loyalty	puts relationships before performance
	bonds with teammates	schmoozes on the job

Metal ▪ **Key word: practicality**. By contrast, the person with a *metal* ladder chooses or is instinctively drawn to people who are strong—competent survivors, tough negotiators, knockabout companions, strategic allies. These friends and coworkers will never fall apart on you, or go soft on you. They'll get the job done, whether it's the "job" of being a reliable, helpful friend or the literal job they're assigned in the workplace. And that's exactly why you chose them—or at least, that's what you tell yourself.

With a metal ladder, you pride yourself on *your own* toughness, practicality, and unsentimentality. Whether because you've endured hardships in your life, or because you're disciplined and ambitious, you like to think of yourself as someone who puts survival, advancement, and advantage ahead of sentiment. But sometimes this is a defense against a secret softness of heart. You may love someone, yet feel compelled to justify your bond with them on the basis of their personal strengths, their wealth or connections, and/or what they can do for you.

You may also pride yourself on your ability to move on, not look back, and acquire a new set of companions wherever you go. This is particularly true if your Ladder is **aluminum**. Aluminum ladders are lightweight and just about interchangeable. You can pick one up at any hardware store, and no matter how battered or paint-spattered it gets, it never acquires the personalized sheen of wear a wooden ladder does. Aluminum Ladders often belong to people who "travel light," who can change jobs, friends, or locations without too much pain. The vagaries of their lives (like an army brat's, a foreign correspondent's, or an immigrant's) may have forced them to become this way.

Iron ladders are more tenacious and permanent. If your Ladder is iron, we bet you've got some very strong, loyal allies—"heavyweights" both physically and in their character. Don't mess with *them*. A **wrought-iron** Ladder, with the lovely tracery of a New Orleans French Quarter balcony, indicates that you surround yourself with people who are cultured and artistic, but tough and indestructible, too. A **steel** Ladder is as strong and weighty as iron, but as bright and impersonal as aluminum. You have an industrial-strength connection right now, but one without much history or (necessarily) loyalty, one that may last only as long as the mutual advantage. (Or maybe you just have a good friend named Steele!) A **gold** Ladder certainly means you treasure your closest friends and work associates, but there's often some material advantage lurking in there, too—they're wealthy, or celebrated, or they can do something priceless for you. A **silver** Ladder (or one described as silver-colored) is as close as a purely metal Ladder comes to combining strength with sentiment.

Here are some of the things a metal Ladder may reflect about *you:*

	Positive	**Negative**
Among friends	chooses wisely	chooses coolly
	relies on friends	uses friends
	returns the favor	unsympathetic to weakness
	builds a strong community	can move on
At work	stresses performance	impersonal
	chooses reliable people	demands too much

excellent networker
builds a strong organization

good downsizer
views people as
stepping stones to success

Rope ▪ Key word: mobility. People whose Ladders are rope are usually mobile, adventurous, and nomadic. They are independent people who travel a lot, or work in freelance fields like consulting. Because they're always coming and going, they need their relationships to be *portable*, like a ship's rope ladder that can be rolled up and taken along, and also *flexible*, giving them plenty of "rope," slack, play. Freedom of movement is their prime requirement. They won't get along well with friends who can't handle long-distance friendship, or employers and colleagues who expect them to stay in one place.

But while rope is flexible, it's also strong and tough—a "tie that binds." It can keep people connected across great gaps of time and space and extremes of weather. Like the rope joining separate mountain climbers, it's a lifeline and a grapevine, passing along bundles of vital provisions and news of far-flung friends. Rope can survive storms as well as metal and better than wood. Soaked in the waters of grief, it only gets stronger. Judging from friends whose rope Ladders hang down from heaven, it may even bridge the gap between life and death. A rope Ladder hanging down from the sky also suggests providential escape or rescue—again, a lifeline.

When the rope Ladder is hanging *on* the Cube, it may mean that others depend on you ("de-pendent" means literally "hanging from"), or that you let in a chosen few and then pull the ladder up, like Rapunzel's hair. A friend in Japan, whose rope Ladder hung from her floating yellow Cube, said she knew her Ladder was her best friend because the rope had loops as grips for climbing, and they were harsh and scratchy and hurt her hands. Her friend can be abrasive, and over their twenty-year friendship they have both fought with and clung to each other.

Some of the qualities you may find in people with rope Ladders:

	Positive	Negative
Among friends	attached for life	far away
	will save your life	out of touch for long periods
	will give you freedom	must be free to leave at will
At work	adventurous	restless
	versatile	dilettantish
	independent	detached

For Ladders made of more un-ladderlike materials, such as water, stone, or plastic, see the materials section for the Cube (page 188–198). Combination Ladders—rope Ladders with wooden rungs, wooden Ladders with iron rungs or metal fastenings—can be readily understood by consulting and combining the preceding sections.

Other types of Ladders we've seen with some frequency include the following:

Branches ▪ **Key word: funky**. A Ladder made of natural branches, often bound together with leather thongs, suggests a Green outlook and a taste for friends and associates who are alternative, craftsmanlike, countrified, resourceful, and unpretentious. (An exception was a Holocaust survivor, for whom a lying-down Ladder of dead branches that had "no connection with the Cube" clearly signified friends and family who had perished.)

Cut into the Cube ▪ **Key word: sibling**. A person whose Ladder is nothing but steps or hand- and footholds cut into the side of the Cube "keeps it in the family"—is best friends with, and/or in business with, flesh and blood.

Extension ladder ▪ **Key word: reserves**. This person always has *more* friends and friends of friends to call on when necessary. Everything he or she will ever need can be found within one or two degrees of separation.

Paint-spattered ▪ **Key word: collaboration**. A Ladder spattered with paint is one you work with; it's marked by the memories of every job. This signifies friends who are also creative collaborators. Actor Willem Dafoe, who works and lives with an experimental theater troupe and has many friends in the movies, has a bright-yellow, paint-spattered stepLadder.

Spiral staircase ▪ **Key words: on-again, off-again**. It looks like a lovely, graceful variation on the Ladder, but the meaning of a spiral staircase has made itself quite clear to us, and it's not so pretty. It's your pattern to have periodic fallings-out with friends and associates. The same cast of characters may be in your life for years, but they're now in, now out of your favor. This may be a quirk of your own, or it may register painful experiences with people who've proven unreliable, fickle, devious, or untrustworthy.

Stepladder ▪ **Key words: independence; duality**. A single Ladder may lean on the Cube, lie down, or be stuck upright in the sand, but a stepLadder, even a folded one, is built to stand on its own. You prefer friends and coworkers who have their own means of support and don't need to lean on you. And/or, the two halves of the Ladder may indicate that you have two distinct sets of friends (as Dafoe does), or that you are close to a couple.

Two ladders ▪ **Key word: duality**. Two Ladders show that the person makes a clear distinction between close friends and acquaintances, or between "work friends" and personal friends. A freelance editor had one Ladder inside his Cube—the friends in his heart—and another one outside but leaning on it, his congenial colleagues and social circle. A literary agent had both a wooden Ladder lying down near the Cube and an aluminum Ladder propped upright against it: private friends for companionship only, professional contacts to advance her career.

POSITION

If your Ladder's material shows how and with whom you like to interact, its *placement* relative to the Cube shows how close you like to get to them. It's a graphic printout of your need and capacity for intimacy, support, companionship, and cooperation, at one end of the spectrum, and freedom, independence, solitude, and personal space at the other.

Anthropologists studying body language in city parks have discovered that there are enormous cultural differences in how close people stand and how often they touch while talking to each other. During the hour a researcher observed them, Anglo-Saxon family members made physical contact all of twice, Hispanics over a hundered times! Similarly, an American talking with someone from India will feel that the Indian is standing too close, while the Indian can't understand why the American keeps backing away; walk down a street in New York and you'll be rudely jostled, while on an equally crowded street in Tokyo people will melt around you, each sealed in a bubble of privacy. Where we draw our body's boundaries, and how close people can come without trespassing, depends largely on the culture and family in which we grew up.

As with bodies, so with souls. When it comes to the balance of closeness and "space" we need in our lives, each of us has our own "culture," our native comfort zone. It's this that the Ladder's position makes visible. Some of us can't imagine the Ladder anywhere but leaning on the Cube. Others want the Ladder close by but not touching, and still others put it way far off.

When we try to live or work with people whose "spatial" needs are very different, we're as likely to misunderstand and wound each other as the Indian and American described above. Between friends, one with a free-standing Ladder may feel crowded by one with a leaning Ladder and back off, trying to restore space, which makes the other feel rejected and attempt to restore closeness. It's a classic vicious cycle and, of course, one that plays out even more intensely and painfully between lovers. Knowing where someone's Ladder stands can help take the sting out of such crossed signals. Once you *see* how you differ, it's easier to give the other person the strokes or the freedom he or she needs. (With a new lover, the position of the Ladder can often give better forewarning of a "spatial" mismatch than the Horse, because people's normal boundaries dissolve in the throes of infatuation—but they'll be back.)

At work, the distance between Ladder and Cube diagrams how closely you like to cooperate and collaborate with others—whether you'll thrive in a crowded workplace or whether you belong out on the road or alone in the studio. Combine this information with the Cube's and the Ladder's relative height, and you'll see whether someone is best suited to be a leader or a follower, a team player or a solo entrepreneur.

You can use the information gained from your Ladder to make positive changes in your life in three ways:

1. Compare Ladder placements with coworkers and friends to better understand one another's "spatial" behavior.
2. Change your job description, or your interactions with friends, to more closely correspond to the position of your Ladder. Or, conversely:

3. Try regarding your Ladder placement as a *diagnosis* of what's bothering you, rather than a *prescription*. Is the Ladder that's leaning on your Cube weighing heavily on you? Does your faraway Ladder make you aware of your loneliness? Would you like more support from those lying-down friends? Other positions are possible. This one may be *characteristic* of you, but it is not *immutable*. Now that you see it clearly, the choice is yours.

LEANING ON THE CUBE

Mottoes: *"In touch," "Lean on me"*
Key words: *easy intimacy, mutual support*
With the Ladder in this position, you're a "people person."

Positives:	▪ You like to be close and involved with others; you take that for granted as natural and comfortable.
	▪ You expect both to give and to receive help and support.
	▪ You're physically affectionate with friends and family.
Negatives:	▪ You may lean on others, or be overly sociable.
	▪ You may take on too many responsibilities, as for aging parents, others' projects, volunteering, etc.
At work:	▪ You're a "team player." You don't like to work alone.
	▪ You don't mind supervision and reporting requirements.
	▪ You like having responsibility for others.

The ladder is how you get on top of the cube:

- You see the support or collaboration of others as essential for reaching your "personal best."
- Friends and coworkers give you perspective, a broader view.

The ladder is how you get inside the cube:

- You only reveal your inner self to the people closest to you.

STANDING INDEPENDENTLY

Near the Cube:

Mottoes: *"Stand by me—but stand on your own two feet!"*
Key words: *closeness with independence*

Positives:	■ You're available, committed, companionable, yet self-reliant.
	■ You are there when others need you—*if* they don't overdo it.
Negatives:	■ You don't like asking for help.
	■ You may recoil inwardly when others need help.
At work:	■ You like to work around others, but independently.
	■ You are self-directed and need to be given autonomy.
	■ You prefer to be responsible for your own work, not to manage others.

- You prefer a horizontal structure—you collaborate well with independent equals.

The ladder is standing straight up:

- You gravitate to people who are self-made and self-reliant.

The ladder is free-standing, at an angle:

- You like unusual or progressive viewpoints, nonconformity, even eccentricity.

The ladder is a stepladder or leans on a tree or landform:

- You seek out people with their own resources or support systems who won't lean on *you*.

The ladder leans against a flowering or fruit-bearing tree:

- Rewards will come to you through promoting the success of others. (A book editor saw a polished library ladder leaning against a date palm: her authors!)

Away from the Cube:
Motto: *"Don't fence me in."*
Key words: *distant, private, self-sufficient*

The more distance there is between the Cube and the Ladder, the more "space" you need. (At an extreme, we've known people who won't even put their Cube and Ladder in the same picture!) If the distance is great, you're a loner.

Positives:
- You're content to see friends occasionally.
- You enjoy your own company.

	▪ You can take care of yourself.
Negatives:	▪ You *only* take care of yourself.
	▪ You may be fearful of closeness. You may be lonely.
	▪ The need for freedom can make you unpredictable and unreliable. Appointments and expectations give you claustrophobia.
At work:	▪ Definitely not a team player.
	▪ You prefer remote or occasional supervision—or none at all.
	▪ You like the freedom to report in once in a blue moon (if ever) and to be incommunicado for long intervals.
	▪ You'll do best as a sole proprietor, freelancer, artist, private investigator, independent contractor, or traveling sales rep.

CONNECTING A FLOATING CUBE TO THE GROUND

Motto: *"Tie me down!"*
Key words: *grounding the Visionary*

You're a consummate idea person—artist, thinker, idealist, dreamer. But you are in danger of floating away into your dream world—or hopelessly botching your practical affairs—unless you're protected and freed by more practical friends and coworkers (with Cubes seated firmly on the ground) to dream, create, philosophize, invent, or imagine.

Positives: You depend on others to

- keep you in touch with practical and financial reality.
- take care of vital but mundane tasks (keep track of time and money, buy groceries, cook meals, write budgets, order supplies, etc.).
- turn your good ideas into useful realities and gently wean you from your bad ones.

Negatives:

- You're the original absentminded professor.
- Allowed to handle practical, financial, or material details, you can make an awful mess.

At work:

- You can be a great collaborator in the right role.
- You depend on and are grateful to others; in turn, you inspire them.
- You need *mental* freedom and *practical* structure and coddling.

◎

LYING DOWN

Motto: *"Low expectations"*
Key words: *hanging out, comfort, slackers*

It's rare to see a metal Ladder lying down (unless its owner specifies that "I can pick it up and prop it against the Cube whenever I need to"). This is almost always a wooden Ladder, and it has an ambivalent meaning, hovering between deep comfort with friends or coworkers and a faint contempt for them.

Positives:	▪ You do not expect others to help you reach your goals because:
	a) you're a do-it-yourselfer, or
	b) it's against your principles to "use" friends.
	▪ You depend on friends only for solace, companionship, and after-hours fun.
Negatives:	▪ You do not expect others to help you reach your goals because:
	a) you view those close to you as useless, or
	b) you don't *have* goals.
	▪ You may choose friends who are unworthy of you—the "king among bums" syndrome.
	▪ You may have friends who are ill, down-and-out, or in trouble.
	▪ You yourself may be a bit of a slacker or party animal.
	▪ You may look down on those who seem less ambitious.
At work:	▪ You don't expect much from the people you work with (often a self-fulfilling prophecy).
	▪ You don't delegate, but feel that to get it done right you have to do it yourself.
	▪ You may be dissatisfied with your job or coworkers. (Time to move up from McDonald's.)

INSIDE THE CUBE

Motto: *"I've got you (under my skin)."*
Key words: *trust, merging, possessiveness*

This position can represent a friend or friends so close and trusted they are "in your heart," a part of you; and/or it can indicate a desire to possess, overprotect, and control others.

Positives:	■ There is someone in your life you trust completely.
	■ You share everything with those closest to you.
	■ Their business is your business. Their enemies are your enemies.
Negatives:	■ You may be *too* trusting.
	■ You may deny the differences between you and others, assuming they think and feel as you do. If so:
	■ You are threatened by disagreement and shattered by betrayal.
	■ You may want to possess and control those around you.
At work:	■ You are a loyal and devoted employee.
	■ You are possessive and protective of those who work for you.

DESCENDING UNDERGROUND

Motto: *"Welcome to the mysteries."*
Key words: *hidden, illicit, subconscious*

This is a rare and intriguing position we haven't seen often enough to fully understand. Friends or coworkers leading you into the underground? It suggests either:

- illegal occupations, scams, or tax dodges;
- transgressive art, culture, or fun;
- guidance into the depths of the psyche (as in therapy, ritual, or deep confiding); or
- a strong connection to someone who's died.

We would welcome contributions to our understanding of this position.

SIZE

The approximate **number of rungs** on your Ladder is an almost comically accurate measure of the size of your inner circle. If you made two lists of the people who *really* matter to you, personally and professionally, we bet each would have about as many names as your ladder has rungs.

Your Ladder's **height** only has meaning relative to the height of the Cube. It reveals whether you are a natural leader (or lonely giant); most comfortable with your equals; or a willing helper, follower, or admirer of superior people.

@

SAME HEIGHT (OR CLOSE TO IT)

Motto: *"Democratic vistas"*
Key word: *equality*

You prefer to be friends with and to work with others on an equal basis. (Slight differences in the height of the cube and ladder suggest whether, among peers, you are more the admirer or admired.)

Positives: You will tend to
- gravitate to those close to you in intelligence, talent, income, power, and/or education.
- play down the differences that do exist.
- give others the benefit of the doubt and assume they *are* your equals.
- believe you're worth as much as anyone on earth—no more, no less.

Negatives:
- Equality may translate as a certain sameness in your inner circle.

- Where differences are undeniable, you may react to your lessers with guilt and your betters with envy.

At work:
- You treat subordinates with respect and encourage them to advance.
- You expect the same from those above you (and are offended if it's not forthcoming).
- You cooperate well with those on your own level.
- You are uncomfortable exercising power over others.

SHORTER THAN THE CUBE

Motto: *"Head and shoulders above the crowd"*
Key words: *dominance, influence, leadership*

In some way, though you may not consciously admit it (it's democracy's last taboo), you feel "bigger than" or dominant over those around you. (Of course, you may be choosing your friends or coworkers for that purpose and avoiding your betters.) They, too, recognize this, and defer or look up to you.

Positives: One or more of the following will be true:
- you *know* you are brighter than most people around you;
- you have thoughts of a lonely complexity that others can't share;

- you have a dominant personality or a big ego; or
- you are very confident of your own value.
- You may use these qualities to be a good leader, or . . .

Negatives:
- You may be superior, a secret snob, domineering, or self-absorbed.

At work:
- In a team setting, you will naturally initiate and lead.
- You will gravitate toward higher management and/or prominence in your field.
- If the Ladder is close to the Cube, you are a generous and protective supervisor or mentor.
- You make a restless and insubordinate subordinate, constantly tempted to exceed your authority and challenge others.

TALLER THAN THE CUBE

Motto: *"Friends in high places"*
Key words: *admiration, humility, service, opportunism*

Goethe wrote, "Confronted with persons of superior merit, the only way of saving one's ego is by love." But *you* don't feel at all competitive with "persons of superior merit." Rather, your way of saving ego is by association. Being close and indispensable to the gifted and/or powerful gives you pleasure and purpose, inspiration, opportunity, and protection.

Positives:	■ You prefer to be around people you can look up to and admire.
	■ Your own Cube may be quite large, but you'll make the Ladder even taller.
	■ When the ladder goes up out of sight, you like to have a powerful "rabbi" or protector—"friends in high places." (Or you may feel strongly that "Somebody up there likes me.")
Negatives:	■ You may be a bit of a name-dropper or power groupie.
	■ You may get your self-respect from who you know, not who you are.
	■ You may tend to be deferential to the great, and dismissive of the ordinary.
At work:	■ You make an excellent assistant, agent, advisor, or facilitator to power.
	■ You can genuinely respect, serve, and further others.

One of our favorite examples of this pattern is power publisher Judith Regan, whose best-selling authors include Rush Limbaugh, Howard Stern, Christopher Darden, and Robert Bork. She described her Cube as "Glowing; bright orange; bright yellow; reflecting from all sides; shiny; jewel-like. Large; right on the horizon, in the middle, centrally located. Brilliant, perfectly shaped, Oz-like." You'd think that would be hard to top—but get a load of her Ladder: "It's leaning against the Cube on the right-hand side. It is bedecked in emeralds and rubies and diamonds. And it's much higher than the Cube. It goes on and on and on, up through the clouds into the sky."

■

The Ladder, of course, only maps one sector of your heart's magnetic field. Intimate relationships are the other side of the story. And there's no relationship more intimate than the one you share with your Horse—as desert dwellers knew very well: They used to take their Arabians into their tents with them. (Of course, sometimes you find yourself in bed with a camel. But that's not as bad as it sounds, as we will see.)

A beautiful, muscled animal you can wrap your legs around—what better image could there be for your lover?

CHAPTER 14

SECRETS
OF THE HORSE

W hen the Horse enters, your Desert—your life!—comes alive. What has seemed a timeless still life suddenly becomes a moving, mortal drama. The Horse upsets things, actually. Unlike the rather stable Cube and Ladder (you'll always have yourself, and friends are forever), this creature could run away. And it needs food and water. So worry and responsibility enter the picture, and unpredictability, and wildness, and breath-catching beauty, and the rhythms of the body. Like falling in love.

But a horse is not *only* erotic. It's also domestic—a workhorse (remember Mick Jagger singing "Wanna be/your beast of burden"?) and a companion animal. It can take you farther than you could go alone, carry you when you're tired, and help you pull your load in life. So it's also your life partner. Once again, the Cube masters have found an image that can say many things in one.

The Horse isn't hard to interpret, as long as you keep in mind that there can be a time lag in the psyche. *It* doesn't always let go when *you* do. When the soul settles on someone, apparently it settles in for the long haul, just like it says in the marriage vows—a poignant discovery in this age of "starter marriages" and no-fault divorce. So if you don't see a resemblance between your current lover and your Horse, take a look at whether it isn't the spitting image of a lost love or an ex-spouse.

That does *not* mean you don't love the one you're with, nor—if your lover's Horse is a palomino, and you're raven-haired—does it mean he or she still actively pines for another. It just means the roots of the old relationship aren't out yet, even though the tree has been chopped down. The deep psyche lives in biological, not electronic, time. It is bound to stately cycles of life, death, decomposition, and regeneration. It cannot channel-surf. That's just a fact.

Of course, there are people who won't settle for just one Horse. When you say, "There's a horse in the desert, describe it," they'll say (decisively), "No, there are several," or (plaintively), "Do I only get one?" Someone with multiple horses certainly *can* (with effort) maintain a monogamous relationship, but he or she will probably always have a polygamous imagination.

Brace yourself for the sting of truth if you play the Cube with your lover, or cube a couple together. It's like compressed couples therapy: Each partner's true view of the relationship will be revealed with unsparing (and often comic) honesty. If your relationship's in good shape, you'll be amused and touched by what you see; if it's going through rough times, you'll "get the picture" of your lover's grievances—one that can be worth a thousand words. Is the Horse (you) remote from your lover's Cube? Is its back turned? Does it freak out or run away when the Storm comes? She or he is feeling abandoned or unsupported—something that may touch you as a graphic image, where a verbal accusation or demand would have made you defensive. In turn, *your* Horse lets your lover look into your heart and see where it hurts. It can start you talking with each other in a new way.

We were meeting a husband and wife and their two preteen daughters for the first time. He was an advertising executive, she a homemaker and full-time mom. While the girls played in another room, their parents sat side by side across the dining-room table from us and played the Cube.

Her Cube was a glass vase on a pedestal, its shape wavy rather than square. (We know what we think[1], but try out *your* interpretive skills on that one.) His was much larger, Plexiglass, sitting on the sand. Her white Horse was busily running around in some dunes way in the background. His white Horse was running towards his Cube. Her Flowers (we know, we're getting ahead of ourselves) were in the vase. He, at first, could not see any Flowers. Then he said, "Oh—okay. They're on the horse's reins."

When we had finished cubing them, and we got to "The Horse is your lover," she turned to her husband and half-laughed, half-wailed, "Oh, that's so *sad!!*" Not knowing them, we thought this might be the typical picture of a workaholic husband and father whose professional preoccupations kept him distant from the family. (He and she both agree that the Flowers—their

---

[1] *Receptive, nurturing, fragile, uncertain, faithful, Principled to the point of loneliness. Committed to being a good wife and mother; feeling a bit inadequate at it.*

daughters—are *her* responsibility.) But later, after the couple had gone home, the people who'd introduced us said that this man often entertains himself alone, too, going out solo to evening movies and cultural events. (And what about those sexy nudes—er, dunes—his wife thinks he's rolling around in?) *He* doesn't feel alone; he perceives (no doubt accurately) that his wife is oriented toward him. But now, he's seen his absence through her eyes. And she's been startled into revealing her pain and indignation.

Will anything change?

Besides portraying a real-life lover or mate as seen through *your* mind's eye—a highly subjective view—the Horse can also represent your lover archetype. H. G. Wells called it "the Lover-Shadow": that unique inner image of a soul mate that begins to form at a very early age, perhaps distilled from a few haunting gestures of a parent (or perhaps from some even more mysterious source), then gathers and deepens through reading and movies, crushes and dreams, till one day we're sure we *see* that image walking toward us, and we fall in love.

Such an image is the template for most of our romantic choices, even though no real person ever exactly fits it. It explains a lot about the repeating patterns in our love lives, and it can help to explain the struggles between lovers when each tries to fit the other into an invisible, unrecognized mold. Knowing each other's Horses can bring those hidden specifications to light. (Your authors confess: Annie, whose dark Horse dodges its own private tornado, has always been drawn to storm-tossed men; Slobodan, whose mare, you may recall, peed on his huge Cube, is still waiting for the woman strong enough to be suitably unimpressed.)

WHAT KIND OF HORSE IS IT?

Your Horse's breed, color, and sex (this last should not be taken literally) evokes the looks and temperament of your lover (real or ideal, present, past, or hoped for) *as seen through your eyes*. It may do this literally or symbolically (or both): For instance, if your horse is shining black, your lover may have dark coloring, and/or may hold the appeal of mystery and romance. A Thoroughbred might represent a lean, tall, long-legged person; a blue-blood; or someone who's intensely competitive, determined to win.

Don't think it doesn't count if the first Horse you see is a real horse you knew in your childhood. That's just a sign of deep comfort with your lover, as if you've known each other forever. Besides, everybody knows that (for girls, anyway) the love of horses in late childhood is a rehearsal. Your lover should be flattered to be compared to your first love!

One thing that's amusing, if not exactly flattering, is the way older people will often describe their Horse—quite frankly—as spavined, swaybacked, lame, or showing other signs of wear and tear. The unconscious isn't cruel, but it is honest, unlike our cosmetic, euphemistic youth culture.

Arabian ▪ **Key words: elegant fire**. This person combines an attractive delicacy with an underlying endurance and fire. He or she is sensitive, refined, intense, intelligent, and high-strung.

Black ▪ **Key words: romantic passion**. A dark-haired or dark-complected lover; someone who has "black moods"; and/or someone with whom you share a powerful, romantic sexual bond (which always involves elements of night and mystery).

Brown, bay ▪ Key words: normality, warmth. Most people think of brown or reddish-brown as "regular horse color," so the lover portrayed—often a brunette or a redhead—is usually also a regular guy or gal, familial, reliable, and stable. Earthy colors can also signify warmth and physical affection.

Camel ▪ Key words: endurance, in it for the long haul. We never *offer* the option of any animal but a horse, but if a camel is what shows up, we've got to accept it. People who see a camel usually think they're just being logical—"We're in the desert, aren't we?"—but in fact, they're portraying their view of their lover as accurately as anyone else. A camel may not be a very romantic image, but it's one of fidelity, familiarity, and reliance—if also of cranky, balky self-will. You have your battles, but you also have a solid partnership that's going the distance, and a rock of a partner who can take whatever life dishes out.

Chestnut ▪ Key words: warmth, passion, temper. Same as brown or bay, above—except the redder the shade, the hotter the temperament.

Donkey, mule ▪ Key words: affectionate exasperation. You see your mate as a stubborn, ornery cuss. Like the camel, it's usually someone you've been with for a long time, long enough for the romance and illusions to have worn off. There's more than a little "familiarity breeds contempt" here. Maybe you were annoyed the day you got cubed.

Flying (Pegasus) ▪ **Key word: transport**. Your lover "takes you away" into a realm of magical happiness. This is often someone you're newly in love with, or feel is the person of your dreams. (But it could also be someone who's literally up in the air: One man's "flying" lover was a flight attendant, and another's wife was on her way across country on the red-eye when he got cubed.)

Gray ▪ **Key words: cool, mature**. Someone with a pale complexion or "a touch of gray," and/or a person who is cool, poised, and reserved. WASPy, where a red-brown Horse is more apt to be ethnic.

Jumper ▪ **Key word: achievement**. A disciplined performer who seeks out challenges.

Mare ▪ **Key words: motherly, sensitive, temperamental, female**. The gender of your Horse does not necessarily represent the gender of your lover. A man can appear as a mare if what you seek in a lover is sensitivity and nurturing (or any other qualities fairly or unfairly labeled "feminine"). Note: It's almost always impossible to tell from someone's Cube whether they're gay or straight—or even male or female (a testament to the androgyny of the soul). We did hear about one woman who'd just come out as a lesbian, whose Horse was (honest to God) *fighting a snake in a tree!*

Multiple horses ▪ **Key words: a roving eye**. A person with four or five horses may simply be dating several people, playing the field. A whole *herd* of horses, however, should send up a red flag: This is an incorrigible womanizer (or man-izer, but this is naturally more common among men. Ever see a mare with a herd of stallions?). After this person has sown enough wild oats, he *may* be able to settle down and confine all further straying to the eyeballs. But don't count on it.

Mustang ▪ **Key word: streetwise**. A tough, scrappy survivor; self-reliant, defiant, untamed.

Palomino ▪ **Key word: golden**. A blonde; a California type—sunny, breezy, casual; or a "golden girl" or guy, attractive and fortunate.

Pinto, paint (spotted) ▪ **Key word: contrasts**. A lover with dark hair and a pale complexion; someone with a crazy patchwork of interests and experiences (even a "checkered past"), or with strong dark and light moods.

Pony ▪ **Key word: pet**. A physically small person; cute, lovable, or unthreatening; not particularly useful.

Stallion ▪ **Key words: bold, dominant, assertive, adventurous** —regardless of gender. When a straight man's Horse is a stallion, you'll find that he likes an independent, daring, feisty woman.

Thoroughbred ▪ **Key word: competition**. Someone who looks and/or acts like a racehorse. Physically, a model type; professionally, on a fast track.

Two horses ▪ **Key words: torn between two lovers**. You (or your lover, if he/she is the one with the two Horses) may actually have affections divided between two people, or between two very different *types* of people. This does not necessarily signal an affair; one Horse may be a past, deceased, or fantasy lover to whom you remain faithful in spirit while sharing your life with today's flesh-and-blood lover. This need not be harmful to the present relationship, and—especially in the case of Visionaries—may even be helpful for it as long as that second Horse stays stabled in the imagination.

Unicorn ▪ **Key words: purity, enchantment**. You see your lover as a magical creature, powerfully innocent and otherworldly. (One woman whose husband portrayed her as a unicorn saw herself as a Cube of cloud.)

White ▪ **Key word: idealization**. Someone you put on a pedestal and look up to, your "knight (or damsel) on a white horse" (also: pale-skinned, blond).

Workhorse ▪ **Key word: responsibility**. This is the kind of horse that pulls the Budweiser wagon: Shire or Clydesdale—powerful, broad-backed, bucket-hooved. Perhaps big and strong physically, certainly strong of character—someone you can rely on—this lover "pulls his or her weight," and then some, when it comes to making a living and taking care of things. May be a workaholic, or sustaining a family or business singlehandedly.

❧

SADDLE, BRIDLE, OR NONE?

Whether or not your horse is saddled and/or bridled indicates which is currently uppermost in your relationship—the practical and domestic, or the passionate and erotic. Of course, these two are not mutually exclusive. But many relationships put more emphasis on one or the other, and most relationships shift their emphasis in different phases. Couples who are the busy parents of young children are the most likely to see each other as "working partners." Later on, when the kids are grown, they may get out of harness and go for a good roll in the pasture again.

Plain leather tack ▪ **Key word: domestic**. A horse wearing a bridle and/or saddle has been tamed and trained, and is being put to practical (if also pleasurable) use. No longer running wild and browsing idly, he or she has learned regular, structured paces, and stays "on track." "Bridle" can also be a pun for "bridal." When you see one on a grazing horse, you know it belongs to someone; it's sort of the equine equivalent of a wedding ring. So the Horse portrayed this way is almost always a spouse (though not all spouses are portrayed this way). And it's a spouse seen through matter-of-factly possessive and practical eyes.

Your lover is "in harness," a worker and responsible breadwinner.

You're busy partners, facing the world side by side right now more than gazing at each other. A bridle suggests that your lover has subordinated impulse and whim to the steady pursuit of shared goals. A saddle suggests comfortable sexual habit and lack of abandon. In general, saddle and bridle represent the comfort and security of marital bonds and roles. (Yuppies seem to prefer English saddles; working-class folks lean toward Western.)

A naked horse ▪ Key word: erotic. If your Horse has no saddle or bridle, it suggests freedom, wildness, trust, lack of control, and sensuality. Married or not, if you see your lover this way, his or her freedom is a matter of principle and pleasure to you—if also a source of anxiety. You don't want your lover to stay with you because you made a vow or signed a piece of paper, but because she or he loves you and chooses you anew each day. Sex and companionship are your reasons for being together, not promises or obligations.

This is the style of relationship that came in with the baby-boom generation, and as erotic and idealistic as it is, it's also associated with a high divorce rate. The unbridled Horse can run away. The very wildness and freedom that turns you on carries a risk. Accept that risk, if you choose it, consciously and willingly. For better or worse, it's how most people live today.

Fancy trappings ▪ Key word: romantic. A kind of compromise or reconciliation of the two above is to adorn your Horse in the royal trappings of medieval or Ottoman nobility: tooled and colored leather, embossed metal and chain mail, jewels, tassels, bells, and feathers. This is the chivalrous view of love and marriage held by an old-fashioned, gallant man, or a woman who reads romance novels. You imagine your lover as a knight in shining armor or a princess in a tower whom you had to court and win. The proposal was the climactic moment in a long, suspenseful story. Your wedding was (or will be) a really big deal, and the memory and sentiment of it will stay fresh for fifty years.

The only problem with this view of love is that it can remain a fantasy. If you won't settle for less than an actual knight, prince, or princess, you're probably still single. It takes a certain kind of shrewd, sentimental imagination to dress up a real person in Cecil B. DeMille costume and pretend your daily bread is wedding cake. (It helps if your lover has some genuinely noble or exotic traits. Two American women spring to mind whose Horses wear glorious trappings. Coincidentally or not, both their husbands are European, and have accents and military backgrounds.)

◉

WHERE IS THE HORSE, AND WHAT IS IT DOING?

You're about to see the truth of your relationship in a nutshell—*your* truth, that is. Your Horse's distance and behavior show what *you* think is going on. To get the whole picture, you must factor in your lover's Horse.

We all know and accept, in the abstract, that each of us sees the world differently. That truism only becomes a shock when we're looking at the same object close up—and it's an "object" of the utmost subjective importance to us both: our shared relationship. It can happen that you and your lover almost seem to be in different loves, different beds. The differences can be benign, even complementary, or they can pose a threat. A difference in two people's perceptions and preferences is fine—in fact, it's inevitable— just so long as both are getting enough of what they need. The Cube cannot create problems between you and your lover. If a problem is there, you'll recognize it the moment you see it. And then you can decide together whether to work on it or accept it. Nothing that's real is ever perfect; some problems, too, are here to stay.

Standing by the Cube ▪ **Key words: commitment, companionship**. You and your lover are close, physically and emotionally. He or she isn't going anywhere (at least, so you assume). You feel confident, comfortable, and secure in the relationship. You are very much a part of each other's daily lives, unlike some couples who may be just as devoted, yet lead quite separate existences.

But what if your lover has a Horse that's more distant from the Cube? The other party to the relationship doesn't feel it's as close as you do. You may be taking him or her for granted, not giving as much as you're getting. But before you change your ways, consider whether your lover *likes* it that way. Perhaps your very assumption of closeness allows him or her a needed inner freedom. Sometimes one member of a couple "does" intimacy for them both. That's fine; just make sure your assumptions aren't blinding you to some potentially serious growing apart.

Don't have a lover? Then this is the relationship you're dreaming of and holding out for. It is the kind you can and will create. Don't settle for less.

Tied to the Cube ▪ Key words: hitched, bound. A man we know felt terrible when we revealed that his Horse, which he'd tied up to a post by his Cube, was his wife. "Oh, no!" he protested. "I don't want to deprive her of her freedom!" He was very relieved to hear that he'd simply invoked the old pun, "hitched." On the other hand, this man—who lost his first wife to cancer—doesn't deny that he is emotionally dependent on his wife and wants her near him. And there's no question that she finds that both deeply touching and, at times, limiting. But then, that's the kind of trade-off being "hitched" is all about.

Circling the Cube ▪ Key words: satellite, guardian. You perceive your lover's life as revolving around you. You're a man, right? Well, maybe not. But it takes a woman of unusual ego to put herself at the center of the universe; it's mostly men who see things this way. This will no doubt elicit ironic groans from our female readers. But, women, be honest: Consider the extent to which it's true, or to which you at least let him *believe* it's true.

"Circling the Cube" can also indicate vigilance. The Horse may be your protector, keeping itself between you and the Storm and other dangers. Or, on a more sinister note, it could be keeping the world away, patrolling the perimeter, ringing you with invisible prison walls of possessiveness. "Revolving around you" can be a double-edged sword. Ever heard of being possessed by your possessions?

On top of the Cube ▪ Key words: supported, honored, dominant, hostage. Oddly enough—or not—it's usually men who put the Horse on top of the Cube. (One rather dominated woman saw her Horse standing *over* her small Cube, framing its universe, but that's different.) It's a sign of gallantry, sometimes even of the ultimate gallantry: acknowledgment of a woman's superiority. Plenty of men *do* support their lovers, and not just financially these days: You may be blessed with a lover who generously encourages your career, and takes personal pride in your accomplishments. He may even put you forward as the family star.

On the other hand, maybe he just puts you up on an old-fashioned pedestal where you can't quite get down and walk on the earth yourself. In the Victorian era, don't forget, to honor women was to confine them. One young man we cubed had his Horse up on top of his stone Cube—screaming to get down! He was aware that his obsessiveness in love had frightened women.

Sometimes, if the Horse is on top of your Cube, you're maintaining a monument or altar in your mind to a lost love. A sad footnote to this position is the man we cubed whose Horse was a gilded statue, with his Cube as its base. He had been passionately in love with his wife, but in recent years a chronic illness had left her overweight and unable to make love—as immobile as that statue. It was as if his life were a monument to the golden memory of what once had been.

Licking the Cube ■ Key words: affectionate, demonstrative. Just as oddly, this is a predominantly female variation. We don't know why: You'd think guys would like being licked, too. Maybe it reflects women's awareness that men, from infancy on, come to them seeking nourishment and refreshment. Often, but not always, this is a melting ice Cube that gives the Horse something to drink in the desert. No matter what your Cube is made of, you're blessed with a lover who shows affection. He (or more rarely, she) is physically demonstrative and probably sexy, too.

Inside the Cube ▪ Key words: fantasy, fusion, possession. It's one thing to invite the Horse inside the Cube when the Storm comes (see the next chapter), quite another if the Horse is pent up in the Cube from the get go. (We see this very rarely.) Any Horse who's this deep in your heart is a fantasy, though it may also represent a real lover whom you've (con)fused all too completely with your Lover-Shadow. This can only work at the very beginning of a love affair—or in the wildest *folie à deux*. Otherwise, you're probably far too possessive, and your real lover is likely to rebel.

More commonly, though, this is a "dream lover," either a fantasy or a cherished memory. A warning: That Horse in your heart may be preventing you from forming a less perfect but more tangible union.

Near the Ladder ▪ Key word: friends. This means that you consider your lover your friend. He or she may have been a friend *before* you fell in love, or you may have been in love long enough to *become* friends. You may also believe friendship is the goal love should ultimately aspire to. You wouldn't be far wrong.

Being ridden by you ▪ Key words: inseparable, "You and me against the world," self-reliance. Even when you're *not* with your lover, your lover is with you. Wherever you go, you point out things in your imagination, and you can't wait to get home and tell him or her. But you'd rather travel together. You dare to go places with your lover where you wouldn't go alone—even places in your own psyche. (It was dark inside one woman's city-block-sized Cube, but on her black Horse's back she wasn't afraid to go in.)

If you don't have a lover, yet you are riding your Horse, you have learned to be your own companion. You may also have an imaginary friend, or the ever-present memory of someone who's become a part of you.

Being ridden by someone else ▪ Key words: inner-directed, "Go your own way." Don't jump to the conclusion that you're being cheated on. The rider could be a parent or mentor who helped set your partner's life direction. (One man said, "My horse has lost its rider"; his wife's influential mother had just died.) Most likely, though, the rider is a part of your lover: a will of his or her own. You're involved with a self-directed, independent person who's going his or her own way no matter what.

One man of our acquaintance saw *two* horses, one ridden by a man, one by a woman. Knowing his wife, we wonder if he isn't subconsciously aware that she is—at least in fantasy—bisexual.

Lying down ▪ Key words: relaxed, lazy, tired, ill, weak. It all depends on *why* your Horse is lying down. Is your lover nesting and feeling at home, "lying down on the job," or just taking a much-needed break?

Acting up (scared by the storm) ▪ **Key words: high-strung, in crisis**. Your lover is easily upset, nervous, tends to lose it in a crisis, or is just having a hard time right now.

In the background ▪ **Key words: a life of his/her own**. Many people of both sexes see the Horse running by in the background, or silhouetted against the sky ("high-profile") as it runs along the horizon. This signifies a lover who is busy and preoccupied with his or her own concerns, usually career or profession.

Leaving the picture ▪ **Key words: "Breaking up is hard to do."** This means just what it says: The relationship, and your lover, is on the way out. She or he may be leaving you, or it may be your love that is leaving.

Grazing ▪ **Key words: nourished, devouring**. When the Horse is grazing near the Cube, it signifies a lover who is getting support and sustenance from you—emotionally, economically, or both. If the Horse is grazing at a distance, you want or have a lover who is fairly self-sufficient, with his or her own interests and resources. If the horse is munching your Flowers, however, he or she may be a drain on your attention or your bank account.

Hungry/thirsty ▪ **Key words: starving for affection**. Your lover is not getting enough love and attention from you, and on some level, you know it.

Dead ▪ **Key words: "It's too late, baby."** Sometimes this is literally the Horse of a widowed person. More often, it memorializes a past ("dead") relationship, or a present one in which the love has died. (One man we cubed, though, was a rather perverse sculptor of found objects who insisted on arranging everything into a still life—apparently, including his wife. His Cube was a slatted crate full of plastic flowers, and his Horse was a skeleton in the sand. That was a few years ago. They're still together.)

No Horse ▪ **Key word: solitary**. This goes deeper than just not having a lover. It indicates a soul that knows no mate. One man we cubed was in a long-running, committed relationship, yet he didn't see a Horse. Even after many years, he and his girlfriend spent no more than two or three nights a week together, and for reasons unknown, he *would not* marry her—or anyone. (And her? Talk about hungry and thirsty—she *ate* her Horse!) However, this story has something of a happy ending: It's one of those cases where someone takes his Cube to heart. Stricken by the unintended cruelty of his revelation (he was cubed in front of her), this man has consciously redoubled his attention, affection, and expressiveness toward his girlfriend. They still aren't married, but she isn't starving anymore.

A comic variation on this theme was an oft-divorced Australian wild man of a karate master who saw no Horse—just a whole lot of hoofprints in the sand . . .

Inanimate Horses ▪ **Key words: unsatisfactory, plaything**. This is taking the phrase "love *object*" a little too literally. A wooden horse or a toy horse is unresponsive and undemanding, and that can be either sad or safe. Having an inanimate horse may be a warning sign of loneliness or dissatisfaction; it can also indicate a need to control the relationship, to move the other person around without his or her answering back. One possible exception is a **merry-go-round horse**, which is festive and nostalgic and could portray a lover you like to have fun with. But merry-go-round horses are out of place in the desert, and they're often chipped and faded and antique; there's a sadness about them, too, an aura of lost innocence and ghostly laughter.

A late friend of ours, who'd pretty much given up on finding someone due to his health problems, said his Horse was a **wooden sawhorse**—a bleak, depressed, but sadly accurate estimate of his chances. A woman we cubed over the radio described a dopey little **cartoon horse** sitting in a heap; she said she'd recently gotten out of a really bad relationship. Our dentist saw the **Trojan horse**, which would seem to suggest suspicion of betrayal (unless his wife was just pregnant).

■

Now, your relationship with your Horse gets put to the test. The Storm is coming!

"Marriages [and relationships] in the long term make it or fail to make it based on how they deal with stress, conflict, and change," says University of California, Berkeley psychologist Robert W. Levenson, Ph.D., who's studied hundreds of couples. "When everything is going along on an even keel, the only issue is whether or not you love each other, care for each other, and whether your union provides some benefits, economic, safety, or emotional. But when there's a challenge—*those* are the real points of vulnerability for [relationships].

"In the course of life, the blows keep coming. It's like a crucible where external sources of heat are constantly being applied. And couples make it or break it, not on whether they loved each other when they started out, but on how skilled they become at dealing with conflicts. Each crisis is an opportunity either to become closer or to become more distant."

Will your Horse stand by you when the Storm comes, or will it run away? For that matter, how is your Cube going to weather it? You'll have to find out sooner or later; in this way, too, the Cube is true to life. Just as it wouldn't be a desert without storms, it wouldn't be life without trouble, challenge, and change.

CHAPTER 15

SECRETS
OF THE STORM

◎

No one really has to be told what the Storm means. A thousand clichés allude to it, from "Into every life a little rain must fall" to "You-know-what happens" (usually hitting the fan in the process). But our ways of reacting to the Storm's turmoil and challenge, destruction and renewal could not differ more. Just as some people will run outside to dance in the rain and dare the lightning while others feel like crawling under the bed with the dog—and still others just close the windows—so our feelings about the storms of life range from terror to dismissal and from anticipatory anxiety to exultant glee.

This part of the Cube is like Doppler radar. What kind of Storm you see, *where* in your desert you see it, and how you feel about it—is it insignificant, threatening, exciting, devastating, or good for the harvest?—provide an accu-weather map of your psyche's relationship to trouble. Of course, it may show the storm tracks of *past* trouble and how it's changed your life. But it can also be useful for forecasting:

- *Where* is trouble in your life right now? Off the radar screen completely, in the future, lurking nearby, buffeting people close to you, or right here?
- What's your "trouble type"? Do you tend to experience personal and professional crises—and react to them—in the form of clouds, rain, wind, thunder, lightning, tornadoes, or sandstorms?
- How does trouble affect you? Does your Cube weather storms well, or does it take a beating? And if so, what kind of beating? Does it get soaked, flooded, battered, buried, or blown away?
- When trouble hits your home or workplace, is it your first impulse to protect others, or to turn to them for help? Do you all look out for each other, or is it everyone for him- or herself?

Note that the Storm is not entirely negative; it can even be a blessing in disguise. Water is nourishing; wind and thunder are exciting (if you know the *I Ching*, you'll remember that thunder is called "The Arousing"); sandstorms sculpt dunes of composure and grace; lightning can strike revelation as well as shock into your heart. Besides, even the worst Storms pass. And often they're followed by rainbows of hope and prosperity and Flowers of creative renewal. People who didn't ask for the storms in their lives, yet managed to wrest new strength and wisdom from them, will often sum up their Storm in one bittersweet, beautiful image: a black funnel cloud whirling on top of a black metal Cube (a sculptor who focuses his mental turmoil into creative force); a dune with two red tulips growing on it where a mirrored Cube used to be (the end of her marriage buried this woman's compulsion to please and released her sensuality and creativity).

And then there are those amazing folks on the flying trapeze who *did* ask for the storms in their lives. "I *love* trouble," said one cool, nervy guy whose business schemes we can only describe as Machiavellian. He was delighted when the Storm left his huge ice Cube "snowed under": Now he could ski down the sides! (Come to think of it, "snow jobs" *were* one of his specialties.) Movers and shakers, trouble-seekers and trouble-makers, such daredevils can often become quite successful. They're not only unusually able (in the words of one) to "take lemons and make lemonade," they *grow* lemons to make sure they'll have a steady supply of their favorite drink. They take trouble as a challenge, and love a good fight. The more cautious among us can only watch them and shake our heads with wonder.

Loving storms, however, is only one marker of likely success. *No* storm—refusing immediately and unequivocally to have one in your desert at all—is another. And a third is any scenario in which the Storm is somehow controlled by the Cube. For instance, singer-songwriter Judy Collins said that her Storm, a tornado, "stays put . . . in the upper left corner." After we decoded the game she said, "I'm a great believer in the fact that we all have trouble and that we must keep ourselves distant from it. I mean, we must know it's there, and we must understand that it's ours, but we don't have to get into an uproar." Her Storm didn't touch the cozy workshop, complete with a mountain view, a blank page, a Mont Blanc pen, and a bagel, *inside* her transparent Cube.

Maybe "success" isn't precisely the right word here: "will" is. However you like it—stormy or serene—that's how you're going to have it, when and where *you* want it. When unavoidable trouble strikes (Collins's son committed suicide), you'll acknowledge it as a worthy adversary, and fight it to a draw or hold it at bay. Control over the Storm shows an extraordinary belief in your power to fulfill your vision, despite everything life can throw at you. That's a belief that tends to be a self-fulfilling prophecy.

❂

WHAT KIND OF STORM IS IT?

Bad weather, like trouble, comes in many varieties. It may be wet or dry, still or windy, icy or tropical, dramatic or just dreary. So it is with the conflicts, losses, and upheavals that are the Storms of our lives. Foul weather provides a rich language of metaphor both for the inevitable buffetings we take from life and for our own "tempestuous" (see?) emotions in a crisis, for there are inner as well as outer Storms. With a little thought and free association, you'll recognize the trouble that assails your Cube in the guise of thunder and lightning, freezing snow, or stinging, smothering sand.

Keep in mind, as always, that you may have personal associations to your Storm that differ from the common patterns described below.

Clouds ▪ Key words: depression, apprehension. Dark clouds may represent dark moods (yours, or those of someone close to you), or they can convey a sense of foreboding, a worry that trouble is on the way. You will know whether this is a realistic assessment of your situation or just a habit of worrying. Some of us are alarmists who *always* feel like dark clouds are gathering and the sky is about to fall. Do your apprehensions often "cry wolf," or do they have a track record of coming true?

Obviously, these two meanings are closely related: Depressed people are often apprehensive, and nothing brings on that feeling of impending doom like knowing a dark mood is gathering in your lover or your boss.

Rain ▪ Key words: sadness, grief, discouragement. Rain obviously suggests tears, but it also has the sense of "Don't rain on my parade" and "dampening one's spirits." When the rain just *falls*, like in Seattle, without thunder or wind, there can be a feeling of gentleness and compassion about it (Shakespeare's "quality of mercy" that "falleth as the gentle rain from heaven"), but it can also convey helplessness or passivity, perhaps acceptance of what can't be changed. When we cubed her a year or two after she was treated for breast cancer, Gloria Steinem's Storm was this kind of rain, intermittently starting and stopping.

When rain comes in torrents, mixed with thunder, lightning, and wind, you don't accept your troubles, you fight back. Whatever it is you may have lost—a promotion, a job, a parent, a marriage—sadness is mixed with the energy of defiance and denial. It has a more cleansing, cathartic quality and is more often followed by a dramatic breakthrough of sunlight, rainbows, and flowers.

A funny footnote: One sixteen-year-old boy told us his storm was *acid* rain, and it was eating away his ice Cube. Of course, when you're sixteen it's important to be cool, but your cool is under constant attack by the gnawing anxieties of school and social life.

Wind ▪ Key words: opposition, opportunity. Wind is energizing, exciting, and *pushy*. It makes you feel like raising your sails and setting forth. But since you're on foot (or horseback) here in the desert, you'll have to push against the wind to make progress, like Jacob wrestling with an invisible angel.

Wind is challenging opposition, either from another person or from the general climate of the time, and it's also your assertive, argumentative way of rising to that challenge. Since wind is spirit (*pneuma* means both in Greek), there may be a heady, bracing intellectual contest or controversy involved, or a war of words, but not a personally angry one—more a matter of principle. In private life, you may enjoy having spirited arguments with your lover or friends.

There are three possible outcomes to your joust with the wind. First, you can stand your ground and let it blow itself out. Second, if you know "which way the wind is blowing" in your household or workplace, the market or the culture, you can turn it to your advantage and sail home. But finally, if you miscalculate, you may literally be "blown away." That's what happened to the Cube—a die—of a high roller we know who gambled on market conditions and lost his business.

Thunder ▪ Key words: conflict, anger. Thunder is an argument that turns to shouting; it's open conflict between people, whether it involves you or is merely within earshot. When you hear the disgruntled grumbling of thunder without lightning, often its bark is worse than its bite, and it's "full of sound and fury, signifying nothing." Perhaps there's someone in your environment who yells a lot, or maybe you're the one who is angry. Noise can be a harmless way of releasing stress and frustration, but remember that to some people it is very frightening. Naturally, it inspires a fear of being struck by lightning, whether or not that's a real possibility.

Lightning ▪ Key words: flashpoint, breakthrough. Lightning "strikes," and so may the person, or the problem, whose rumbling wasn't just an empty threat. Thunder and lightning together can be a dangerous combination. But unless the Storm is right on top of you, the risk is small—and many people find it exhilarating. Full-fledged thunder and lightning storms are often described as beautiful and exciting by people who fearlessly enjoy the dramatic emotions of life lived to the hilt.

But lightning also carries the meaning of inspiration and enlightenment. Sometimes it's the friction of conflict that strikes that spark, and a brilliant flash of insight illuminates what was in darkness before. That's why some people work best in violent "storms," finding their inspiration in the midst of turmoil and danger. And sometimes conflict gives rise to its own resolution, which could not have been reached without the electric charge built up by a fight. An example is the way the shock of the O. J. Simpson verdict illuminated the unbridgeable gulf between black and white Americans—and so allowed many whites, for the first time, to glimpse the other side.

Heat lightning, without thunder, suggests tension, mental restlessness, or obsessive rumination.

Tornadoes ▪ **Key words: unpredictable violence, trauma**. A tornado is tragedy that strikes suddenly, without warning. Whether it's illness, death, or disaster, it's the most destructive and freakish kind of trouble life can throw at you. You don't usually see it coming, so if there's a tornado in *your* desert, the worst has probably already happened, either to you or someone near you. Or you may have been deeply affected by some violent tragedy out there in society, as reported on the news.

A tornado can also represent a dangerously troubled person, and the destructive forces in his or her psyche. It often portrays something like post-traumatic stress syndrome—the persistent memory and aftereffects of severe trauma in the past. Annie saw her Horse being chased by a tornado, and of course she is married to a man who was taken from his family at age sixteen and imprisoned in the Gulag. It's certainly a trauma that has pursued him ever since, although—like Annie's Horse—he dodges it nimbly.

Dust devils ▪ **Key words: annoyances, psychological quirks**. A dust devil is like a harmless little pet tornado—a minor problem in your life or psyche that is merely annoying, and sometimes even almost endearing. It may be something (or someone) that bothered you a lot in the past, but then you "got its number" and drained it of its menace, and now it's just a shadow of its former self. It's not surprising that dust devils often seem to be the only Storm left in the deserts of older and wiser people. They portray the way we ultimately learn to live with our own defanged neuroses, the small imperfections of life, and the exasperating quirks of our companions.

Sandstorms ▪ Key words: confusing, painful, overwhelming. If your Storm is a sandstorm, your style of reacting to trouble probably has been to lose your bearings and your perspective. When a crisis hits you can feel blinded, trapped in your subjectivity, unable to see beyond the end of your own nose. The stuff comes at you so stingingly fast that you can only blunder around trying to cover your exposed sensitivities. You feel humiliated, mocked, flayed. You can get overwhelmed by your problems, buried under them. Yet the paradox is that the curves of drifted sand left by the Storm are prettier and more interesting than a plain Cube. The shape formed by you and life together is a more subtle one. The edges of your ego have been softened by trouble, and perhaps so has its hard shine.

Snowstorms ▪ Key word: windfall. We haven't seen many snow-Storms, and those we have seen so far have been positive. They've come to the rescue of ice Cubes imperiled by the desert heat, and provided a substance almost like manna—soft, cooling, refreshing, a source of water to drink, a material to sculpt into fun and useful shapes, a surface to ski on. Snow turns the ground into virgin territory that you'll be the first to tread, taking pride in your crisp footprints. In other words, if your Storm is snow, you most likely see trouble as an invigorating opportunity.

Rainbows ▪ **Key words: relief, hope, success**. A rainbow is a smile after tears (or in the midst of them); like flowers, a rainbow represents relief and reward, the recompense for conflict. And that recompense is not always intangible: Don't forget the legend of the pot of gold! People who are willing to go into battle for what they want often get it. As best-selling publisher and storm lover Judith Regan put it, "Out of the storms in *my* life have come the rainbows."

❀

WHERE IS THE STORM?

Your Storm's location in your desert tells you where trouble is in your life—behind you, ahead of you, right here, far away—but also where trouble is in your mind: Is it something you brood on daily, or do you say, like Scarlett O'Hara, "I'll think about it tomorrow"? Chronic worriers and pessimistic realists always see the Storm coming. Even when things are going well, they'll say, "It isn't here . . . *yet*." Optimists and people with killer guardian angels may see it, too, but they say, "It's gonna pass us by." Blithe deniers don't see it at all: They say, "What storm?" People who really *are* in trouble right now see the Storm hit their Cube, but so do those who thrive on risk and conflict; their image is an invitation: " 'Blow winds, and crack your cheeks! Rage, blow!' "

Behind you or behind the Cube ▪ **Key word: past**. You've been through some major trouble, but it's definitely over now. You are rebuilding, and you're stronger and wiser for the experience, if also scarred by it. You feel that "the worst is over" and that nothing will ever be able to throw you like that again. (The first person who ever told us, "The storm is behind me," was a recovering alcoholic with eight years of sobriety.)

Coming closer ■ **Key words: approaching, threatening**. (See "Clouds," page 261.) There may be real problems headed your way, in which case, at least you've got time to brace yourself and prepare. You see it coming; you won't be caught by surprise. On the other hand, you may just be a pessimist or a worrier. That can be due either to temperament or past experience, or both. Some people are chronically apprehensive even though nothing really bad has happened to them; some are mistrustful and vigilant because life has hurt them before.

Here, Now ■ **Key words: present, recent**. If the Storm actually comes right through your scene, you're either embroiled in trouble or conflict right now, or you just were not long ago. You can assess how well you're holding up by the condition of your Cube. (See "How does the Storm affect . . ." below.) Of course, if you're a storm lover, you're in your element.

Inside the Cube ■ **Key words: inner turmoil**. This is perhaps the single most frightening place for the Storm to be. We've heard this one from prisoners and troubled adolescents. It shows that whatever bad things have happened in your life, you've taken them inside you, and they have become you. Now storms are brewing in there. You're like a pressure cooker. If you don't find a safe outlet soon, the whole thing could blow. It's a warning signal, even a cry for help.

On the horizon ▪ Key words: "Somewhere out there is one with my name on it." If your Storm is in sight, but not menacing the Cube or its companions, you have a realistic awareness that trouble is an omnipresent possibility (and for many others, of course, a present reality), as well as an ultimate inevitability. *Some* kind of trouble lies in wait for all of us. This is an objective truth. Some people thrive by ignoring the fact; some ward it off by obsessing about it. You keep one eye on it, but it doesn't stop you from enjoying life.

Out of Sight ▪ Key words: good fortune, denial. Don't see a Storm at all? Your motto is "Out of sight, out of mind." You're not in trouble right now, lucky you, so you're not going to think about it. You're not going to waste too much anguish or pity on other people's problems, either. After all, they are often self-created. You may be a little bit of a "looking out for number one" type. On the other hand, you just may be really, really happy or serene or successful right now. Who can blame you for wanting to enjoy it, unalloyed?

❦

HOW DOES THE STORM AFFECT THE CUBE, LADDER, AND HORSE?

When the Storm appears, what happens to your desert scene? The answer may range all the way from "Nothing" to "Total devastation" ("The Storm totally remakes the landscape," said a Holocaust survivor with a sweep of her hand) to "The desert bursts into bloom." A cube standing flat on the ground is a very stable form, and Realist Cubes, in particular, seem to come through most Storms unscathed. Among people who've taken recent direct hits, however—such as divorce or the death of a parent—we've seen Cubes that flooded, sank, blew away, got struck by lightning, pitted by scouring sand, or buried under sand dunes.

Perhaps most revealing are the interactions, alliances, and abandonments that go on between Cube, Ladder, and Horse in response to the Storm. Trouble is the acid test, not just of your lover, but of the mettle and reliability of the others closest to you. Who's "the strong one" in your circle of family, coworkers, and friends? Are you usually the one others turn to in times of trouble? Have they been there for you when you really needed them? Your Cube knows.

As you read through these possible effects of the Storm, you may feel that several are true of you. The one in your Cube vision is the one your deep mind has chosen to emphasize, the message it most wants to send you. **Blown away** means exactly what it says (see "Wind," page 262): You are ambushed, vanquished, devastated. If the Cube stands firm but the Ladder is blown away, your friends or associates are the ones having problems, or you perceive yourself as stronger and steadier than they are in a crisis.

Buried under sand means your troubles have been overwhelming—and have altered the landscape of your life. A buried Ladder is someone close to you who's either in deep doo-doo, or lost to you.

Erosion or pitting of the Cube by blowing sand or rain suggests that your troubles are eating you up or wearing you down.

Flooding of the Cube means you're filled with emotion.

Horse Freaks Out: Your lover gets upset more easily than you do—or shows it more. Or, he or she is the one having the problems right now. How do you feel about your lover's upset? Protective? Anxious? Annoyed? This is one of the most common ways that opposites attract and conflict: A calm, phlegmatic person seeks the stimulation of a high-strung live wire, who, in turn, needs insulation. They exasperate each other, but they need each other.

Horse huddles by the Cube: Your lover depends on you in a crisis. You feel protective, and perhaps a bit superior or condescending. (In some cases, perhaps, you create the crises so your lover will cling to you.)

Horse/ladder taken inside the Cube: You are protective, generous, and nurturing. You take responsibility for those close to you and share your resources with them in times of trouble.

Horse lies down: Your lover's style is to "lie low" in a crisis and wait for it to blow over. This may be passive and avoidant, or simply calm and sensible.

Horse runs away: You suspect your lover can't be counted on in a crisis, but will either panic or set about saving his/her own skin.

Ladder broken: A friendship or working partnership is disrupted by conflict or calamity.

Ladder hovers over the Cube: You rely on a friend, family member, or mentor as your protector.

Ladder knocked down: You must watch helplessly as those close to you deal with trouble. Though you are stronger or more fortunate right now, you cannot protect them. And you can't rely on *their* support till they get back on their feet.

Ladder sheltered by the Cube: In a crisis, you're the strong one who looks out for your friends or coworkers.

No effect means the trouble isn't really major, and/or everyone is strong enough, separately or together, to get through it in good shape.

Struck by lightning can mean you (or those around you) have suffered a shock or blow—or that you've had a brainstorm. One divorced woman said that lightning had struck and killed the rider of her Horse!

Water damage, wetness represents sadness or grief.

The desert blooms: The most paradoxical, yet natural, effect of the Storm is that it's so often followed by renewal and blossoming. It's a truism that new creation cannot happen until destruction has cleared away the old. Trouble is harrowing, but it can also fertilize your life; you often need to be tested and—dare we say deflowered?—by life before you can really flower. You also need to prove you can take care of yourself before you take on the care of someone or something more tender and vulnerable. When the ground of your being has been turned by the wind, cracked open by thunder and lightning, drenched with rain, and restored to serenity, *then,* and only then, can you grow your garden. You can create, and procreate.

It makes perfect sense that the Flowers come after the Storm.

CHAPTER 16

SECRETS
OF THE FLOWERS

" April showers bring May flowers." So the order in which these objects appear in the desert isn't random. And your Cube vision isn't just a static picture, either. It's a dynamic *story*—your life story. Its dramatic structure is a universal one (albeit a theme with infinite variations): the unfolding of the human life cycle.

The arrival of the Cube, Ladder, Horse, and Flowers actually corresponds to the three great sequential tasks of every adult life—*identity, intimacy,* and *generativity*—as described by the famous psychoanalyst and theorist of human development, Erik H. Erikson, in *The Life Cycle Completed* and other books. Erikson also recognized the Storm. He said that at each stage, with each task, we are tested; each has "its 'natural' crisis," its risk and challenge, its ordeals of loss and learning. And each task we successfully fulfill helps to fortify us, so we can withstand life's inevitable storms without losing heart.

Erikson, best known for coining the phrase "identity crisis," took the understanding of the life cycle a couple of significant steps beyond Freud. Freud had looked mainly at how we relate to our own bodies, sexual drives, and fantasies at different stages of infancy, childhood, and young adulthood. Erikson also looked at how we relate to the world. For example, he said the big drama in the life of a toddler (Freud's "anal" stage) isn't just about toilet training; it's about "me!" and "no!"—about standing on one's own two feet. (Or one's own four corners, as it were, because that's really when your "Cube"—your distinct sense of self—is born.) And adolescence isn't just about raging hormones; it's also about the need to discover who you are.

But we aren't finished products when we reach biological adulthood. Erikson believed we continue to develop through clearly defined, if overlapping, stages all our lives. As soon as we get a grip on who we are (*identity*— the Cube), we start searching for who we're going to love (*intimacy*—the Ladder and the Horse). And joining with others in love, friendship, and work "bears fruit"; it generates new people, wealth, and other creations (hence, *generativity*—the Flowers). Any of these achievements can be thwarted or threatened by Storms—crises of loss, confusion, and failure. (When we avoid intimacy or suffer an estrangement, Erikson speaks of *isolation,* a condition poignantly pictured by a solitary Cube, far from its Ladder, abandoned by its Horse.) Big enough Storms affect who we are, and we go back and start the whole process over.

■

When we first got cubed, we were told simply, "The flowers are children." We had to figure out the rest for ourselves. When cubing parents, of course, there was no problem. But people who had no children (or even *hated* children) still had Flowers, often well-fed ones flourishing close to a protective Cube. "Friends' kids, nieces and nephews, etc." didn't quite do it, though some people thought that's who their Flowers were. How could we account for the fact that a karate master with two small daughters had fields and fields of Flowers behind his Cube? Could it have anything to do with the fact that he is the leader of an international organization with twelve million students? Yes, and a kindergarten or classroom certainly looks like a colorful garden.

It was a short step from that to realizing that doctors and other health caregivers "tend" their patients; agents want their clients' careers to "grow" (one, with no children and no use for them, saw a tall sunflower between her Cube and Ladder, spiraling toward the sun—a good image for ambition); salespeople "cultivate" their contacts and accounts; brokers "grow" their clients' portfolios; lawyers protect their clients from being "eaten alive" by natural enemies . . . and it was only another small step to seeing that the Flowers need not be human (for some of us, they're our pets), or even alive in the strictest sense: ideas, creations, achievements, even investments are also a flowering of our being.

Here's how Erikson puts it: "Generativity . . . encompasses *procreativity, productivity,* and *creativity,* and thus the generation of new beings as well as of new products and new ideas, including a kind of self-generation concerned with further identity development. . . . The new 'virtue' emerging from this . . . namely, Care, is a widening commitment to *take care of* the persons, the products, and the ideas one has learned to *care for.* . . . the young adults' capacity (acquired in the preceding stage of *intimacy* vs. *isolation*) to lose themselves so as to find one another in the meeting of bodies and minds, is apt to lead sooner or later to a vigorous expansion of mutual interests and to a libidinal investment in that which is being generated and cared for together." (That's the "erotic" aspect of the Flowers we mentioned earlier—our visceral, vulnerable, proprietary, and protective feelings toward both our children and our work, not to mention our money.) "Care," Erikson continues, "includes . . . the parental and the didactic, the productive and the curative . . . Genuine generativity, of course, includes a measure of true authority."

A friend of ours puts it more colloquially: "The Flowers are 'your baby,' whatever that is." And if you definitely have more than one "baby"—your kids, your pets, *and* your pet projects—can the same Flowers represent them all? You'll have to decide for yourself whether it's either/or or both/and. If you're sure the Flowers represent just one of those possibilities, then that's the one you're most actively "cultivating" right now. (For example, you may be pouring your heart into a work project now that your kids are pretty well grown.) But we suspect that the Flowers—how many you see, what kind(s), whether they're clustered or scattered, how close to the Cube, Ladder, and Horse they are—can often represent a *style of generativity* that is consistent across your work and family lives.

Some of us are possessive and protective of all our "products" (children, paintings, patients, investments, start-ups), hug them close, and don't like to let them go. For instance, we know a veterinarian whose Cube was a gauzy desert tent, and her Flowers were two red roses in a vase inside the tent. She does have two adopted daughters, and is a very motherly mom to them. But she *also* has turned her office staff and clientele into an extended family, makes house calls, sees pets in her home . . . you get the picture. A young Cube friend from the Net described his Flowers like this: "At the bottom of the cube, along the side facing the westering sun, a single bud forces its way out of the sand. It reaches up about a foot and begins to bloom pure white. Four petals and a stalk, the lonely flower edges closer to the protective cube, which reaches out and envelops the flower in a soft blue light." At twenty-three, Wen-Hung, an aspiring online journalist, doesn't have any kids yet, but he *does* keep all his poems, prose writings, favorite quotes, and good ideas under his wing on his Web page. Chances are some-day he'll be an equally protective daddy.

And then, there are those of us who put our "products" out into the world and trust them to fend for themselves. Mind you, parents of young children, those most actively involved in parenting, *almost never* see their Flowers scattered randomly around (the rare exceptions are—you guessed it—nearly always men). Parents' Flowers are typically few, bright-colored, vividly detailed (seen in close-up), and under the Cube's or Horse's close protection. But some parents *will* plant their Flowers in a special garden, pool, or oasis, or on or under a tree, where they're sheltered, but a bit inde-pendent of the Cube. Perhaps these parents trust life itself to be their *comadre* or *compadre*—or maybe they entrust their kids to day care or a nanny for a good part of the day.

When non-parents, or the parents of grown children, see their Flowers scattered far and wide, certainly it can mean "Other people's kids, not my responsibility," or "Mine have flown the nest." But it may also signify a characteristic attitude toward *work*. Annie saw her desert randomly studded with low, silvery-blue bushes, like sagebrush, that had tiny yellow flowers growing on them. Admittedly, they *were* about cat height, and she *does* have sixteen cats who cheer her up. But the abundance and random distribution of the bushes—with no special relationship to the Cube, as if "they belong to the desert, not to me"—also reflect her attitude toward her work, which is (journalist style) to do it, let it go, and not look back.

"The flowers are *everywhere!*" said novelist Douglas Coupland, summoning up the image of a valley in Africa where "there are trillions, literally trillions of seeds lying dormant in the soil, and then every six or seven years the rain comes and all the flowers germinate and grow at once." The image fit, he said, because "this year's leitmotif is ideas and projects. Like three million trillion of them."

๏

WHAT KIND OF FLOWERS ARE THEY?

There are almost as many different reasons for choosing a particular kind of Flower as there are kinds of flowers to choose from. Your Flowers may physically resemble your children: One woman with three blond kids saw hers as daisies. Or the Flowers may embody your *feelings* toward your children: Red roses suggest a heartfelt, almost romantic parental passion. Or they may symbolize a *quality* you sense and treasure in your child, such as violets for shyness, or lilies for purity.

This is one of the most nonverbal parts of the game, and by far the most difficult to translate into words. Flowers have the power to evoke feelings directly, bypassing the descriptive and analytical parts of the brain. Smelling a flower and feeling its fresh coolness against your face is not unlike nuzzling a child. So the Flowers you choose may simply be your favorite kind, or a kind whose color and form evoke the same feelings in you that your children do. (For some common associations to colors, see page 196.) Multicolored or assorted Flowers show your awareness of your kids' variety and individuality.

When the Flowers represent work, their *type* may be less telling than their *arrangement* (abundant or sparse? around the Cube or all over the place? in clusters or a field?). Different colors indicate that you enjoy a *variety* of students, patients, clients, projects, or interests, which may be all mixed together or neatly planted in separate patches. Flowers all of one kind or color suggest a work life unified by a single aim or theme.

Using flowers as a secret language of sentiment was quite a craze during the Victorian era. The custom had, in fact, followed a path eerily similar to the Cube's: It found its way first into France from eighteenth-century Turkey, where, according to the Reader's Digest book, *Magic and Medicine of Plants*, an English traveler noted that "you may quarrel, reproach, or send letters of passion, friendship, or civility, or even of news, without ever inking your fingers." Victorian lovers would send each other elaborate, specific messages in the form of bouquets. There were experts who specialized in "reading" these flower messages, and who wrote many books "breaking the code," telling which flower signified what sentiment. If the number of flower "dictionaries" on the Internet is any indication, the craze may be making a comeback. Here's a brief gleaning of some of those traditional flower meanings. Many of them could apply equally well to "generative" or romantic love. Some of these meanings may be so embedded in the collective unconscious as to have influenced your choice of Flowers. As always, however, give your own personal associations first priority.

(When a type of flower comes in several colors, the traditional rule for lovers generally seems to be that **red** means love or remembrance; **white** stands for truth or fidelity; and **yellow** signals unrequited love or jealousy.)

Anemone forsaken

Azalea protectiveness; fragile or fleeting passion; Chinese symbol of womanhood

Cactus endurance (In the Cube, we find, cactus Flowers almost always signify children of divorce. They can also be stepchildren, or kids conceived or raised with difficulty of some kind [infertility struggles, domestic conflict, single parenthood, financial hardship, delinquency]. Or they may be work projects that were hard to bring to fruition. In almost every case, the feeling toward the Flowers is "It was worth it.")

Carnation January, the new year; fascination; admiration; "unforgettable" (solid color tells a lover "yes," striped means "no")

Chrysanthemum autumn; leisure; optimism; long life; happiness

Crocus cheerfulness (the first flowers to poke through the snow)

Daffodil "You are the sunshine of my life."

Daisy innocence; purity

Dandelion faithfulness; happiness (and carefree childhood summers)

Forget-me-not true love; memories

Forsythia anticipation

Geranium stupidity; foolishness

Gladiolus sincerity; strength of character (flower of the gladiators)

Iris faith; hope; promise; courage

Lily purity, virginity; motherhood (In the Cube, lilies often seem to represent intellectual or artistic inspiration.)

Lily of the valley sweetness; humility; returning happiness

Marigold cruelty; grief; jealousy

Narcissus vanity, self-absorption

Orchid magnificence; refinement; wisdom; womanhood

Pansy thoughts, ideas (from the French *pensée*)

Petunia resentment and anger, or the soothing of those feelings

Poinsettia festivity

Poppy sleep, oblivion; fantasy

Rose *red:* romance, "heart love"; *white*: spiritual love, secrecy, silence; *yellow*: friendship

Tulip imagination; perfection; luck; fame; beautiful eyes

Violet modesty, simplicity; reciprocated love, faithfulness

Water Lilies devotion

Wildflowers spontaneity, freedom

Zinnia remembrance, constancy, lasting affection even in absence

There are at least two kinds of flowers that occasionally turn up in the Cube that you won't find in any Victorian posy book or 1-800-FLOWERS ad:

Artificial or plastic Flowers This *may* be an emphatic declaration that you don't want children. (As Cube legend has it, one West Coast marriage broke up when his wife's plastic Flowers finally convinced a man who wanted kids that she could not be talked into having them.) In the realm of work, it might mean wanting the appearance of success without the risk and trouble, or it might mean there is a falseness in your relationship to your work—it isn't coming from your heart. In some way, a person with plastic Flowers is protecting himself or herself against the vulnerability that is the price of true generativity. Both our kids *and* our work are "hostages to fortune," flesh of our flesh, full of nerve endings for both pleasure and pain.

Dead Flowers So far, we've never known this to mean dead children (though a woman who had an abortion her boyfriend wanted more than she did saw one Flower being eaten by her Horse): It sometimes seems to mean grown-up or estranged children. For an older woman, it can be a way of saying, "My mothering days are over." To one young karate instructor, the bouquet of dead Flowers laid at the foot of his Cube represented the troubled youths he hopes to work with, kids who feel cut off from their families, as he does. In the realm of work, dead flowers may signify a dead hope or failed project.

The Victorian flower glossaries are fun, but we suspect the real "language of flowers" is an idiolect—a language of one. It's most likely that you "chose" your Flowers (or they chose you) based on something known only to you, perhaps even only to your subconscious mind—a favorite color or scent, a haunting or happy memory. What do the Flowers remind you of?

Where do they take you? Follow the trail of associations to penetrate deeper into the mystery, but never to solve it.

❀

WHERE ARE THE FLOWERS, AND HOW MANY?

The location and abundance of your Flowers will often reveal, among other things, whether you're a parent or not. Certain patterns—a few, bright flowers very close to the Cube—are typical of, though not exclusive to, parents whose children are still in their care. But parent or not, it is the placement of the Flowers that best reveals your "generative style"—how prolific, possessive, and protective you are. Just as some of us have many friendships, and others only a few deep ones, we vary a great deal in how widely or deeply we distribute our creativity and our caring. At work, too, some of us prefer to cultivate a few projects or people in depth, while others can spin off scads of ideas, or lead or entertain masses of people.

By the base of the Cube ▪ Key words: under your wing.
Children: This is the most common position for parents of young children. It means, naturally enough, that you're keeping your kids close, under your shelter, protection, and supervision. The Cube will interpose itself between the Storm and the Flowers, creating a zone of calm and safety for them to grow in.
Work: You take a protective and proprietary attitude toward your clients or creations. You probably keep them close to you even after the job is fin-

ished. If you're an author, for instance, you have a special shelf or bookcase for your own books and their translations; if you're an athlete, you still have every trophy you ever won. Former clients or students may become friends.

Around the Cube ▪ Key words: gather 'round. Very similar to the above, except there are more Flowers, and they completely ring the Cube.

Children: You like a big family, and you like to be surrounded by your brood, in the midst of your clan. At the drop of a hat you'll let your kids invite their friends or cousins over, too, so there's often a lot of happy commotion and kids underfoot in your house. While you shelter the Flowers, there's also a sense that they protect you. You feel safe and significant in the bosom of family.

Work: Your work enhances and defines you. It's the face you present to the world, both an attractant and a subtle defense. This is also a common position for those whose work involves being surrounded by young people— schoolteachers, Little League coaches, and karate teachers, for example.

On top of the Cube ▪ Key words: on your back; from your head.

Children: Your kids are "living on you." They're at home, and you're supporting them, holding them safely above the burning desert sands. Country singer Joe Diffie agreed to be cubed for our first book. His Flowers were "pink and yellow and white. Pretty good-sized. Growin' on top of the cube." He has four kids at home, who were then ages thirteen, ten, five, and three.

Work: You have a fertile mind. Ideas, inspirations, and products are sprouting from your head.

Growing all over the Cube ▪ **Key words: dependent, your pride and joy**.
Children: We have a friend who is rather modest, self-deprecating and self-effacing. All the pride she cannot take in herself, she invests in her son and daughter. She saw her Cube as a drab adobe structure, but when the Flowers came along, blossoming, fruit-bearing vines twined all over it. The Cube supports the Flowers, of course, but it's the Flowers that make the plain Cube beautiful.

Work: This is very much like "Around the Cube." You feel about your work the way our friend feels about her kids. It is both fruition and enhancement; it increases *your* value. You wear your achievements or ideas like jewelry on your being. (For example, we know a young scholar of English literature who has white lilies growing on the sides of his Cube.)

Inside the Cube ▪ **Key words: nurtured, protected, possessed**.
Children: There are at least five possibilities that we've seen:
1. You are pregnant.
2. You're filled with longing for a child.
3. You are very protective of and nurturing to your children, maybe even a little overprotective. Be careful they don't grow up to be hothouse flowers.
4. You're possessive and can't let go. You view your children as a part of you, which can stunt their growth.
5. Your twentysomethings are *still* living at home.

Work: Similarly,
1. You're pregnant with ideas, or incubating a project.
2. You have trouble finishing things and letting them go out into the

world, where they'll be exposed to the weather of public scrutiny. This may cause a creative block.

3. You have a home business.

4. You're possessive of your money.

Cut Flowers in a vase ▪ **Key words: disconnected, on display**.

Children: Cut Flowers can sometimes represent adopted children, or grown children—those who "didn't sprout here" or who have "cut their roots." Nonetheless, having them on display (usually inside or close to the Cube) indicates great parental pride, even bragging.

Work: Your job description may involve taking care of or showcasing someone else's children, products, or pets.

In the foreground ▪ **Key words: first and foremost**.

Children or work: Sometimes the Flowers will be "up front," "in your face," or right at your feet, closer to you—the viewer—even than your Cube. This indicates that whatever your Flowers represent—a child or children, a current project, or young people you are mentoring—is absolutely in the forefront of your life right now, your most pressing priority, more important to you than yourself.

One divorced man who saw a single Flower right up front had his difficult and lively fourteen-year-old daughter living with him for the summer, confronting him with a new challenge every day. Pioneering feminist Gloria Steinem's "field of flowers in the foreground, closer to me than the cube" seemed to represent the younger generations of women she seeks to nurture and encourage.

In a garden or oasis ▪ **Key words: freedom with safety; well-provided-for**.

Children: You've given your kids a rich but safe little world of their own to play in, which can function independently of you (perhaps because it is overseen by your Horse or a nanny). You remember your childhood as an enchanted garden—or you wish it had been—and you are determined to provide your kids with magic memories.

Work: You feel you work in a privileged, hospitable, and supportive environment that nurtures your best efforts.

Under a tree ▪ **Key words: sheltered but independent**.

Children: You trust life itself to protect your children; you feel it's important to give them freedom to discover the world for themselves. And/or you entrust them to someone else's care.

Work: You may have a protective mentor, job security—or sheltered assets!

Growing on a tree ▪ **Key word: miracles**.

Children: So far from taking proprietary pride in your offspring, you are struck by the mystery of their arrival. You agree completely with Kahlil Gibran: "Your children come through you, but not from you; they are the sons and daughters of life's longing for itself."

Work: The ideas and connections you need seem to come to you of their own accord. Your work life has been blessed by synchronicity and serendipity.

Near or on the Ladder ▪ **Key word: friends**.

Children: You regard your kids as your friends, or, the important children in your life are your friends' kids.

Work: Your work is the fruit of close collaboration, inseparable from the people you do it with.

Under the Horse ▪ **Key words: protected by your partner**.

Children: You see them as under the capable protection and authority of your partner. (It's also possible that they could be dominated or overshadowed by your partner.)

One new father saw his Horse "watering" the Flowers—by peeing on them! No offense was intended; that's a perfectly good dream image melding the bodily functions of birth and nursing.

Work: Your efforts are associated with your lover in some way, which may be positive or negative. She or he may be the cocreator or the protector of your work—or may overshadow it and block the sunlight from reaching it.

On the Horse ▪ **Key words: your partner's prize**.

Children: When either sex places the Flowers in a garland around the Horse's neck, it's a sign of a close partnership made closer by shared parenthood (or shared work—see below). A man is acknowledging that his lover has "run and won the race" of giving birth—he was probably there to cheer her, lathered and panting, across the finish line—and that the children are the visible reward for her victory. Then, too, she may be the one who is "carrying" them. (Where the Flowers are in relation to the Cube and the

Horse will often reveal who's doing the lion(ess)'s share of the parenting.) A woman who places the Flowers on the Horse is acknowledging that children have been (or will be) brought into her life by her lover. Indeed, many women view marriage and motherhood as one desirable package. It's not uncommon for women who haven't yet found Mr. Right to picture the Horse and Flowers together, off at a distance from the Cube.

Work: If the Flowers are on the Horse, your achievements are dedicated to or bestowed upon your lover; or, he or she is supporting your work in some way—whether as muse, business partner, collaborator, or most constructive critic.

Eaten by the Horse ▪ Key words: a demanding lover; competition.

This is one of those images, like a pyramid or a camel, that can easily be mistaken for a logical, literal response. "A horse in the desert needs something to eat, right? Well, here come some flowers, just in time!" Sorry, you won't get off so easily. While a Horse grazing on pretty flowers is a peaceful, pastoral image, there's actually a lot of aggression in those grinding jaws.

Children: This suggests that your lover is a big child who "eats up" your nurturing, leaving little or none for actual or hoped-for children. (We've told you about the woman who had an abortion for her lover's sake, then saw her Horse eating her Flower.) Conversely, it could mean that your lover isn't getting enough emotional nourishment from you, and seeks it instead from children—not the best thing in the world for them.

Work: There are several possibilities here. First, it could be that your lover is competing with your work for your attention, and is interfering with your ability to get things done. Or perhaps your lover is living off the fruits of your labors (or spending your money). Or, more benignly, your partner shares your interests or "dines out on" your successes.

Under the Storm ▪ Key words: under a cloud, troubled.

Children: "Troubled children?!" singer-songwriter Tim McGraw said. We were cubing him for our first book and he saw his Flowers under an ominous bank of storm clouds. He admitted there *was* a child in his life—his then girlfriend's five-year-old son, "a great kid" he was obviously fond of. What he didn't tell us (and may not yet have fully known himself) was that the boy was already under the cloud of Tim's impending breakup with his mother.

Work: There is some kind of cloud over your working life—not exactly an uncommon situation in these days of brutal competition and unpredictable downsizing.

Falling from the sky ▪ Key words: inspiration, insemination.

Children: A Receptive woman we cubed saw white flowers falling into her dark cubic pool, and immediately related it to her desire to get pregnant.

Work: A woman writer, with no kids and no intention of having them, felt that the lilies falling from the sky onto her Cube beautifully portrayed the way ideas come to her.

Scattered randomly ▪ Key words: on their own.

Children: They're probably other people's—and of no great interest or immediate concern to you. If you *do* have kids of your own, you're somewhat remote from them right now—preoccupied with your work or other concerns, emotionally distant, or divorced from the parent who has primary custody.

Work: If the Flowers are abundant, all over the place, you are prolific and sow your efforts broadcast, trusting them to make it in the world without your continued vigilance. For instance, you may start up businesses and then let others run them. Or if you write, paint, or make movies or music, your focus is on whatever you're creating right now.

If the Flowers are sparse, small, and indifferently scattered, it can be a sign of discouragement or dissatisfaction with your work, a feeling that it isn't adding up to much—and a signal to think seriously about a job or career change. In what field would you really be "in clover"? What would it take to get there?

In patches ▪ Key words: eclectic, dabbler.

Work: Flowers growing in separate beds or patches belong to someone with many different and distinct interests. We got a comically literal example when we cubed the director of the Learning Annex in New York. His white marble Cube indicated that he likes working with creative people, and his patchwork quilt of Flowers of different kinds and colors resembled nothing so much as . . . a Learning Annex catalog!

In a field ▪ Key words: a faithful following.

Work: A cultivated field of Flowers invariably belongs to a leader, entertainer, or public speaker who has the ability to reach and influence thousands, even millions, of people. CEOs of large organizations often show this pattern, as well as generals in the armed forces, politicians, singer-songwriters who go out on tour, and nationally prominent activists who reach a mass audience with their ideas. Depending on the nature of the enterprise, the Flowers may be planted in uniform, orderly ranks, or they may be as chaotic and multicolored (multicultural) as a sold-out concert venue.

No Flowers ▪ **Key words: childlessness, a dry spell**.

Children: You don't have any, or if you do, they play no part in your daily life. We cubed one long-divorced man in his seventies who insisted that his Flowers were in a separate picture, a whole different part of the desert, from his Cube, Ladder, and Horse.

Work: You know all too well what the poet Gerard Manley Hopkins was going through when he wrote, "Mine, o thou lord of life, send my roots rain." You're in the middle of a creative, spiritual, or financial dry spell. Such droughts do end, but while they last they are very painful, and they *feel* eternal. It may take nothing less than a major Storm to get your life's desert blooming again.

❧

CUBING THE FLOWERS: A NOTE ON PLAYING THE CUBE WITH KIDS

Children age five and older not only love playing the Cube, they can play it again and again. They don't much care what the different images stand for;

they just have fun imagining them. Their imagery is colorful, zany, daring—and startlingly revealing of their loves, conflicts, and fears. Cubing your "Flowers" every now and then can help you cultivate them with more understanding.

Happy kids make their Cubes fearlessly large and whatever bright color or goofy pattern strikes their fancy. Annie's niece Rachel, when she was twelve, made her Cube purple, her favorite color. Her brother Nick, then nine, chose the colors of a ladybug for his Cube. Why not? But if there's something haunting a child, you'll know it. An intense and angry adopted eight-year-old who'd run away from home twice said there was a scorpion inside his Cube. A fatherless boy about to explode into puberty saw everything else—Ladder, Horse, Storm, and Flowers—crammed *inside* his small Cube. A child fighting bone cancer said his Cube was a toy box, and a cactus spit fire at it. The box opened up and spit water back at the cactus!

Two of the images have somewhat different, though related, meanings for a child. The Horse, that passionate love object, almost always represents a parent. (A five-year-old girl whose parents were embroiled in an ugly divorce saw a lion stalking her Horse.) We don't impose that interpretation on a child, though; we just say, "The Horse is someone you love very much." The Flowers often reveal a young child's understanding of biology. One little boy saw a Flower sticking out from under his Horse's tail; he must have just learned where babies come from. The Flowers may also represent sisters or brothers, pets, dolls, drawings, imaginings, or favorite hobbies—the play that is the forerunner of both nurture and work.

At adolescence, kids begin to play the Cube as adults, and they become the authority on their own Cubes. At this time of self-discovery and rapid change, it's good to have a soul mirror, as well as a glass mirror, to peer into. The Cube contains everything that makes this life passage so intense and dramatic: a talisman of your own uniqueness (the Cube); passionate friendships, betrayals and shifting alliances (the Ladder); crushes and first loves (the Horse); whatever's bothering you most (the Storm); the rapid maturation of body and mind—the birth of serious interests, as well as body changes and blossoming sexuality (the Flowers). It's a charming and comic touch that teenagers will often portray the Horse as part cartoon or some impossible color (say, purple with pink polka dots), showing that the idea of a "lover" is not yet quite serious, still far-fetched and fanciful.

On the other hand, it's perfectly possible that their boyfriend or girlfriend has purple hair.

Playing the Cube with your kids completes the cycle, and shows it beginning again. They may still be in your garden, but they've already got their own Cubes. And to visit their newly opened worlds, even more than their rooms, you've got to be invited.

Sometimes—often—we envy kids the freshness of discovering themselves and the world for the first time. We dimly remember how that was, and we're always on the lookout for experiences, songs, places, spells that can revive our sense of wonder. The Cube is one of those. Watch the expression on the face of the next person you cube while he or she describes a Cube you've never seen before. Every time you play, it's the first time.

THE WHOLE
PICTURE

❂

And beyond the Flowers? "Beyond care," wrote Erik H. Erikson, lies "something called *wisdom*," or *integrity*—the sense of coherence and affirmation that comes from finding a meaningful design in the story of your life. The Cube, in the guise of a game, is a tool that helps you to see that design (and reveal it to others), and so to move toward integrity, whether by deepening your acceptance of your current situation or taking steps to change it. "Integrity" is a higher octave of "identity," because it includes so much more than just the self: the world, our work, the people we love, and the next generation. And yet, the characteristic ways in which we reach out, the people we connect with, the contributions and choices we make, even the things that seem to "just happen" to us, are all part of the unfolding of the "vital design" of the self—a design that psychologist James Hillman, in *The Soul's Code*, suggests we bring with us in seed form when we're born. The Cube is you, but so is the arrangement of Ladder, Horse, Storm, and Flowers that makes the Cube's signature "magnetic field" visible and makes your whole desert scene a composition, unified by your character, your destiny, your *style*.

To us, the best thing about getting cubed, and then cubing most of the people we know and most new people we meet, has been this: *We have never seen the same thing twice.* We assumed we knew what "individuality" meant, but this little game has shaken such smug assumptions to their roots, making us irrevocably aware of how much we normally miss, how much more there is to people than we see. An artist really *does* lurk in the soul of every accountant and construction worker—it isn't just a fatuous cliché. No one is boring. Is there someone who makes you yawn, who you think holds no surprises for you? Play the Cube with him or her. We guarantee surprise, or your money back. Play it with someone who annoys the hell out of you. You'll come away with a chastened new appreciation for that person.

The Cube has been used with great success in orientations (not to mention on first dates) as a way of bypassing stereotyped small talk and helping strangers to bond. But play it with everyone in your family or your office, and it will be like meeting those familiar people for the first time. (Learning all too familiar celebrities' Cubes has certainly been like meeting *them* for the first time.) Old bonds dusty with habit, inattention, and misconception can be loosened and retied with more delicacy and precision. You'll begin to feel that you don't *really* know someone, or quite know how to deal with them, till you know their Cube.

But the beginning of wisdom, and the ultimate goal of this ancient game, is the same as those words written over the entrance to the Delphic Oracle: "Know yourself."

THE LEGEND
CONTINUES

BY SLOBODAN D. PEŠIĆ

❧

MARCO POLO AND
THE KNOWLEDGE OF THE CUBE

I know that in the early hours of Tuesday, July 2, 1271, a tall merchant ship well equipped for a long journey left the Adriatic port of Venice on its way to Palestine. The ship with its heavy cargo carried three important passengers. Two of them, brothers and merchants, Nicolo and Mafeo Polo, were well known in the city of Venice for their long journey to China. Inspired more by the fear of competition than actually yearning for trade, this was their second attempt to reach Mongol-occupied China.

The third passenger was a young man of seventeen and the son of Nicolo Polo. His name was Marco.

Usually talkative and cheerful, Marco had been unusually quiet for the past month, and his reasons for this long journey were different. His heart wasn't in the trade; it was at the feet of Katerina de Vilioni, daughter of Domenico de Vilioni, another merchant of Venice and competitor of the

Polos. Six months ago Marco and young Katerina had fallen madly in love and decided to get married. When she asked her father for his blessing, he refused, and instead locked her up in the house. The two decided to run away and secretly marry. Somehow, Domenico de Vilioni learned of his daughter's plan and decided to take her with him on a long-planned journey to the East.

At the beginning of June 1271, his ship left Venice in its own attempt to reach the silk route to China. Katerina was the only woman on board.

■

I know that Nicolo, Mafeo, and Marco, on their way to Palestine, made a brief stop at Korcula, an island in the Adriatic archipelago, where the Polos had a family house and where Marco had been born. They got instructions and some old sailors' advice from Marco's grandfather, who told his grandson: "Although love is the greatest gift of all, I'd rather swim the sea than . . . but never mind. Hopefully you'll learn something on your journey."

■

I know that the ship arrived at the last eastern outpost of Latin Christendom: Acre, Palestine's port in the Mediterranean Sea. The Polos traded some of their goods for horses and camels at the market in Jerusalem and then crossed Arabia, heading to Baghdad. After a brief rest they followed the well-known caravan route across Persia and reached the city of Samarkand.

War was raging between Mongols and Persians outside the city, and the father, the uncle, and the son decided to wait because it was too dangerous to travel farther.

One evening, bored and exchanging stories with other merchants in the market, Nicolo, Mafeo, and Marco met Ali-Fata, a stranger of unknown origin, dressed like a Turkish Sufi, who entertained them with an unusual game called the Cube. He would ask each one present the same very simple questions, and after they responded, he would look into a well-worn booklet and read them the answers.

It was indeed entertaining and revealing and everybody liked the funny little game with its endless answers and precise interpretations, except Marco, who was immensely intrigued and wanted to learn more . . . and asked Ali-Fata to teach him the game. .

Ali-Fata said:

"It's not a game, and you must tell me, why do you want to learn?"

"I am in love and I must find her!"

Ali-Fata looked into his eyes.

"I can see from your answer that you are destined to use it wisely. I can teach you, but I cannot give you the knowledge. I am only the messenger."

In the following months of seemingly never-ending war outside the city of Samarkand, Marco Polo learned Persian, Turkish, Mongolian, and how to interpret the Cube.

■

I know that the Cube was a very simple game; it had only five questions and a seemingly limited numbers of answers. But the more one played the game the more the answers multiplied, and interpretation became impossible unless one searched out the answers in the Book of Cubes.

Marco Polo was so intrigued by this game that there were days when he forgot to eat or sleep or even to think about his beloved Katerina.

■

One day Ali-Fata gave Marco the book and said: "Take the knowledge, and don't forget that you are only the messenger."

■

Three days later and more than a year since the siege of the city had started, the Mongol khan finally won the battle. The new ruler entered the city and asked only one thing: to bring him Ali-Fata. He told him: "You know that the long war has been fought because of you. The only thing I have come for is you. Kublai Khan is waiting, and you must come with me or I'll burn the city."

"Oh, mighty khan, I know that you haven't come to bring me to the great Kublai Khan. You have come to get my knowledge and become the greatest khan of all Mongols. Greater than Chinghiz. Greater than Kublai . . . But I am here to prevent that. My Cube and your Cube are different. I cannot go with you and you will not burn the city."

The khan laughed and said, "How's that?"

"Very simple. In three days I will die. In three days I cannot teach you anything. That's why I trained a young student and passed him my knowledge. Still, it will take him a long time to master the right answers and pass it on to you. Kublai Khan will search and find you before you get the knowledge, and you will lose your head. You must take him to Kublai and thus save yourself and the knowledge."

The khan thought for a moment and said, "I'll wait for three days. If you don't die, I'll kill you and do what I think is best. Now bring me your student."

When Marco was brought to the khan, he asked him, "Do you have the knowledge of the Cube?"

Marco answered, "No, mighty khan, I am only the messenger."

■

After three days Ali-Fata died as he had predicted, and the khan cut his head off. As proof that nobody has the knowledge, the head was put in salt and taken with Marco and his father and uncle on the long road to China. The city of Samarkand was burning behind them.

■

I know that Kublai Khan was a wise man. He understood the chain of events and ordered the rebellious khan to be beheaded. He buried the head of Ali-Fata in his garden and installed Marco as master interpreter of the Cube. He said, "If this youth lives to manhood, he cannot fail to prove himself a man of sound judgment and true worth!"

■

Thus the immense job of collecting, classifying, and understanding Cubes had begun. Soon the villages, cities, provinces, armies—the huge empire of the Mongols—was organized according to the Cube. People from faraway places would be brought to Marco to tell their cubes and were sent to do things according to their answers. . . . During the reign of Kublai Khan, the Mongol empire became the greatest and largest ever in the history of mankind.

Marco had completely forgotten about Katerina. While his father and uncle traveled extensively searching for Cubes, he was confined to his head-quarters in the imperial palace, studying and organizing the ever growing collection of Cubes.

One day, after almost seventeen years spent in the service of the khan (or the Cube), Marco went to Kublai Khan and informed him that the enormous library of deserts, cubes, ladders, horses, and flowers was collected and that the knowledge of the Cube must travel West now.

"You want to go home?" asked Kublai Kahn.

Marco answered, "Yes, for I can see that the greatest khan has mastered the knowledge of the Cube, too."

Kublai Kahn smiled and said, "I am sorry that you are leaving, but we are now destined for different things. One of my daughters is going to be married to a young prince at the far western outpost of my empire. See that she arrives safely at her new palace. This is the last service that I will need from you."

■

I know that Nicolo, Mafeo, and Marco Polo were entrusted with the princess and that they embarked on a long journey from China to India by sea. The fleet numbered fourteen ships and six hundred souls, not counting the seamen. On the long journey Marco entertained the princess and the young women in her royal entourage with the game of the Cube, making them laugh and giggle at his interpretations and accurate guessing of their past and possible future.

After all these years of hard work it was still a pleasure playing the game.

Then, one day of the long journey, the princess said, "I wonder what Katerina's Cube would be?"

Marco opened his eyes.

"Katerina?"

The princess told him a story of a young concubine who had been brought to her and with whom she loved to exchange stories. Her name was Katerina, and her stories were mainly about distant places and love.

"One day she told me the story of a young lover who promised to swim the sea after his love was taken away from him. It was a beautiful story, and I decided to help her find him. I helped her escape from the palace, which was a prison for her. I don't know what happened to her. I wonder what happened to her lover? Do you think he really wanted to swim the sea?"

Marco paused, looking at the calm sea.

"I don't know, my fair princess. I thought that I had mastered the knowledge, and the answer to your question should have been easy. Now I can see that I am only the messenger."

There was a tear in his eye.

■

I know that huge waves and rough seas took a lot of lives on the ships. Only eighteen people survived. The princess was delivered to her destined prince and the Polos continued their journey across Arabia, then by sea back to Venice. Exhausted, humiliated, all of their goods lost or stolen, they stopped again at Korcula to rest and seek some advice from Marco's grandfather. He listened to their stories and said, "Nothing's lost. Sell the knowledge of the Cube to the Duke of Venice."

■

I know that the Polos tried to sell the Cube as advised, but the Duke and the people of Venice preferred oriental spices and China's silk to "games."

A few years later war broke out between the two competing cities of Genoa and Venice, and Marco was imprisoned in Genoa. There, in prison, he again started telling the knowledge of the Cube to willing listeners. One of them was Rustichello of Pisa, a romance writer, who collected this knowledge into the book titled *The Travels.* The other important listener, Giovanni Columbo, was a guard in the prison, and it is known that he paid close attention to Marco's stories.

It is not clear what happened to the original knowledge of the Cube. Some say it was buried next to Ali-Fata's head when Marco Polo decided to leave China. Some say that Marco himself threw it into the sea off the coast of India when he learned that Katerina had been so close to him all those years, and some say that he gave it to his grandfather in Korcula. . . . Some say that the knowledge was lost in subsequent copying of the original Rustichello manuscript. Some say that Giovanni Columbo confiscated it from Marco when he was in prison.

I don't know . . . Many years later, in the summer of 1492, a sailor from Genoa, a great-great-grandson of Giovanni Columbo, the guard of Marco Polo, started a long journey to the West from the coast of Spain. A well-thumbed book of the *Travels of Marco Polo* was in his possession and many believed that he was looking for the Cube. His name was Cristoforo Columbo.

I know that in the summer of 1951, in the city of Yangzhou, East China, a well-preserved tombstone was discovered bearing Franciscan symbols and an elaborate carving of the Madonna. In Gothic script inscribed on the marble one could easily read: "Katerina, daughter of Domenico de Vilioni, died in 1342."

■

I know that the Mongolian Society of Germany and other scholars have recently started questioning the authenticity of Marco Polo's travels. . . . Many inconsistencies and inaccuracies have been found: China's Great Wall, printing, tea . . . were never mentioned in the book.

■

I know that in the summer of 1987 I was cubed for the first time. It happened on Korcula, not very far from the house of Marco Polo.

■

I know . . . I am only the messenger.

S OURCES

❀

(i n t h e o r d e r q u o t e d)

If you'd like to trace our steps back into the history of the Cube, and perhaps venture even further, the following sources will lead you to many others. An Internet search on "**Sacred Geometry**" is also strongly recommended. The many books of **Idries Shah** (only two are listed here by name) are our most trusted source on the Sufis.

CHAPTER 1:

Plato, *Timaeus and Critias*, translated by Desmond Lee. Penguin Books, 1977.

Catherine Yronwode, "The Sacred Landscape," http://www.luckymojo.com /sacredland.html.

R. Klibansky, *Continuity of the Platonic Tradition*, quoted in *Timaeus and Critias,* p. 22.

Tom Kenyon, "Sacred Geometry and the Evolution of Consciousness," http://www.lightworks.com/MonthlyAspectarian/1995/March/ Sacred Geometry.html.

Revelation 11-16: the King James Bible

Frances A. Yates. *Art of Memory*. University of Chicago Press, 1966.

William A. McClung, *The Architecture of Paradise*. University of Chicago Press, 1983.

Idries Shah, *The Sufis*, Introduction by Robert Graves. Doubleday Anchor, 1971.

The Theosophical Society homepage: http://members.aol.com./tstec/hmpage/tsociety.html.

Olcott National Center of the Theosophical Society in America: http://www.theosophical.org./center.html.

Much of the work of Claude Bragdon has been reprinted by Australian composer, philosopher, and Web wizard Diarmuid Pigott on the Claude Bragdon Homepage (a site worth visiting for its beautiful border, based on a Bragdon design): http://shift.merriweb.com.au/books/bragdon/index/html.

Claude Bragdon, *Observations on Dynamic Symmetry* is at http://shift.merriweb.com.au/books/bragdon/b-dynsym.html.

Claude Bragdon, *A Primer of Higher Space* is at http://shift.merriweb.com.au/books/bragdon/b-phs.html. Note: At this writing, only the first part of *A Primer* was on the Bragdon Homepage. The second part, "Man the Square: A Parable of Higher Space," could only be found in libraries, in the edition of *A Primer of Higher Space* published by Alfred A. Knopf in 1923. Check the Bragdon Homepage or E-mail diarmuid@merriweb.com.au to find out if "Man the Square" has been added to the site.

Sigmund Freud, *The Interpretation of Dreams*, Avon Books, 1965.
Alfred O. Mendel, *Personality in Handwriting*, Stephen Daye Press, 1947.

CHAPTER 13:

Idries Shah, *Learning How to Learn: Psychology and Spirituality in the Sufi Way*. Harper & Row, 1981. pp. 153-4.

CHAPTER 14:

University of California psychologist Robert W. Levenson, Ph.D., is quoted, with his permission, from an interview with Annie Gottlieb for an article, "Fighting the Good Fight," that appeared in the May/June 1996 *Mirabella*.

CHAPTER 16:

Erik H. Erikson, *The Life Cycle Completed*, Norton, 1985.
The Magic and Medicine of Plants, Reader's Digest Books, 1986 (the "English Traveler" is quoted, without source, on p. 422).

A C K N O W L E D G M E N T S

Thanks to Big Jacques for in-flight refueling and afterburners, and to Dalma Heyn for oxygen and daffodils.

Thanks to the growing and dedicated crew of "The Cube: The Next Generation":

Arielle Eckstut, our agent, at James Levine Communications;

Laurie Abkemeier, our editor at Hyperion;

Wen-Hung Fang and ScoTT of the Senate, who launched the Cube into cyberspace.

For help in following the tracks of the Cube over the sands of time, special thanks to Teddy Bakewell and Kristin Peterson; the Newberry Library, especially Paul Gehl and John Powell; and on the Web, to Julia Hoerner, Catherine Yronwode, Tom Kenyon, Diarmuid Pigott, and Debi Bliss.

Thanks to Dörthe Binkert, of Scherz Verlag, for her brilliant publishing of *Der Magische Kubus*.

And to Andras Halasz for the only possible images.

Finally, thanks to our families and friends (you know who you are!) for spreading the word but keeping the secret.

About the Authors

ANNIE GOTTLIEB is a New York–based writer specializing in psychology. She is co-author of the bestselling *Wishcraft: How to Get What You Really Want* and (with Slobodan D. Pešić) of *The Cube: Keep the Secret*. Other works include *Do You Believe in Magic? Bringing the Sixties Back Home,* and the text to artist Thomas McKnight's *Voyages to Paradise*. Her journalism has appeared in the *New York Times, Mirabella, Utne Reader, The Nation, New Woman,* and many other national publications. With her partner, writer/actor Jacques Sandulescu, she has studied Kyokushin Karate for over twenty years. They have sixteen cats.

SLOBODAN D. PEŠIĆ is an emigrant or immigrant (depending on the mood), an astrologer, and a provider of second-hand smoke and useless and impractical ideas. A professional observer and a writer/director who has worked for TV and film companies in Europe and the U.S., his first feature, *The Harms Case,* was selected for film festivals in Cannes, Berlin, Jerusalem, Montreal, Toronto, San Francisco, Hong Kong. . . . He lives and works in New York City, where he is developing (as writer/director) an American comedy based on Mikhail Bulgakov's *Heart of a Dog,* and (as producer-cinematographer) the world's first low budget wide-screen epic, *Burn.*